EIGHT DAYS

That Changed the World

A Devotional Study from Palm Sunday to Easter

Don M. Aycock

kregel
PUBLICATIONS

Grand Rapids, MI 49501

Eight Days That Changed the World

Copyright © 1990, 1997 by Don M. Aycock

Published by Kregel Publications, a division of Kregel, Inc., P.O. Box 2607, Grand Rapids, MI 49501. Kregel Publications provides trusted, biblical publications for Christian growth and service. Your comments and suggestions are valued.

All rights reserved. No part of this book may be reproduced, stored in a retrieval system, or transmitted in any form or by any means—electronic, mechanical, photocopy, recording, or otherwise—without written permission of the publisher, except for brief quotations in printed reviews.

Cover design: Alan G. Hartman

Library of Congress Cataloging-in-Publication Data
Aycock, Don M.
  Eight days that changed the world / Don Aycock.
     p.   cm.
     Originally published: Nashville, Tenn.: Broadman Press, 1990.
     Includes bibliographical references.
    1. Jesus Christ—Passion—Meditations. 2. Holy Week—Meditations. I. Title.
BT431.A97   1997   232.96—dc21   96-46394
                                                   CIP

ISBN 0-8254-2142-x

Printed in the United States of America
1 2 3 4 5 / 01 00 99 98 97

To
my wife, Carla,
and my sons, Ryan and Chris,
people who embody the meaning of Easter,
and to
the staff at Baptist Memorial Hospital
and Baptist East Hospital
in Memphis, Tennessee,
partners in healing ministry.

Contents

Introduction

Easter for many Christians seems to be a minor interlude between Christmas and summer vacations. I say that not to be harsh but simply to point out that for many believers, the Easter season has never been emphasized. The church choir has worked hard on its Christmas cantata, and after its performance the members are worn to a frazzle. "You mean you want us to get another cantata ready for Easter?" they ask the choir leader.

While Christmas is a "big" holiday in our nation because of the number of dollars which exchange hands, Christmas should be of less importance to Christians. Here is the foremost affirmation of Christianity and of this book: Easter is the focal point of the Christian church. It commemorates the willing sacrifice of Christ, it identifies those forces that put Him on the cross, and it proclaims the good news that He arose from the dead as a promise to those who would follow Him.

The name *Easter* is not found in the Bible. Scholars think it comes from the name of the Anglo-Saxon goddess of spring who was named Eostre or Ostara. A festival was celebrated on the day of the vernal equinox. Traditions associated with this festival survive in the Easter rabbit which was a symbol of fertility and in colored Easter eggs, another such symbol. These eggs were originally painted with bright colors to represent the sunlight of spring.

Christians should see Easter as the most important day of the year—the day of the resurrection of Jesus Christ. The exact date of Easter is debatable, but the modern method of determining was established by the Council of Nicaea which met in A.D. 325.[1] Nicea ruled that the Easter festival should be celebrated on the first Sunday after the full moon following the vernal equinox. If the full moon should occur on a Sunday and thereby coincide with the Passover festival, Easter would be celebrated the following Sunday.

A discrepancy — called the "epact" — between the solar year and the lunar year caused the problem of determining the date of Easter. This problem with the calendar increased in its discrepancy because of the difference between the true astronomical year and the Julian calendar then in use. Easter can be celebrated in most churches today anytime between March 22 and April 25 inclusive. The Eastern Orthodox Church uses a different method of dating Easter and can observe this holiday as much as five weeks later. Whatever date is chosen, Christians today recognize that the Easter season is vitally important to the development and maturation of their faith.

This book is about the Easter octave — the eight days between Palm Sunday, the day Jesus entered Jerusalem on a donkey, and Easter, the day of Jesus' resurrection. The four Gospels do not match exactly on their perspectives of that last week. John's chronology is slightly different from Matthew's, Mark's, and Luke's. Even so, we can get a fairly good idea about what happened on each day during that unique week.

I have not attempted a verse-by-verse study, nor have I tried to cover every event of Jesus' last week. Instead, I have approached this study synthetically by taking the accounts from all four Gospels and trying to make sense of their reports. The major events of each day are examined with a view toward understanding what happened then and what difference it makes today. Those days were literally eight days that changed the world.

---

1. J. W. C. Ward, The Four Councils (London: The Faith Press, 1951), 15–16.

1

SUNDAY

Entering Jerusalem

Beneath all the great accomplishments of our time there is a deep current of despair. While efficiency and control are the great aspirations of our society, the loneliness, isolation, lack of friendship and intimacy . . . and a deep sense of uselessness fill the hearts of millions of people in our success-oriented world.   —Henri Nouwen

Palm Sunday, Good Friday, and Easter form a three-legged stool upon which the Christian faith rests. The other days in the last week of Jesus' life are like spindles running from one leg to another, supporting and reinforcing them. Remove any one of the three legs, and the whole stool collapses. They stand together, or they fall apart. That is my basic conviction in this book.

Good Friday—the day of Jesus' crucifixion—was not "good" in any traditional sense of the word. We might better call it "Black Friday." Whatever its name, though, it was a time when God opened His arms wide to the world. Easter was the day when all of the pieces of the puzzle came together, and people could see the whole picture.

But Palm Sunday? I do not remember ever hearing that name until I was in college. Some people grow up in churches where a special service on the Sunday before Easter is a well-established tradition. I did not grow up in such a church. Our little church in Louisiana was surrounded by oil-pumping units. They sucked that precious crude out of the ground with regular whirring and swishing regardless of the day or season. The regular momentum inside the church matched that of the outside. Things went along as usual for the most part. We always sang "Low in the Grave He Lay" on Easter, but I do not remember anything else about the season. Easter itself was important, but not much else around that time seemed to matter (except to all of us children who thought Easter was ushered in by a bunny which laid eggs and dropped Hershey's kisses).

I learned later that nothing happens in a vacuum. Every effect has a cause. Good Friday was the effect for which Palm Sunday was the cause. Palm Sunday was the day Jesus rode into Jerusalem on a donkey and said by His action, "This is what God is all about!"

Those last eight days from Sunday to Sunday, that Easter octave, changed the world. Later generations called it "Holy Week." It is so important that the first three Gospels devote one-third of their precious little space in telling about it. John gave about one-half of his pages to it. That ratio gives us a clue to the week's importance.

Jesus Comes to Town

Jesus, with His disciples and other followers, rode into Jerusalem on that fateful Sunday. Luke tells us that much earlier Jesus had "set His face" to go to Jerusalem (Luke 9:51, KJV). That means that He had made up His mind to go because He had important business there. He allowed nothing to stop Him, although He did pause here and there. One such pause was in Bethany, a sleepy village about two mile east of Jerusalem.

Mary, Martha, and Lazarus lived in Bethany. Jesus stayed with these dear friends instead of trying to find accommodations in Jerusalem. Thousands of pilgrims thronged into that city during the Feast of the Passover. Jerusalem tripled its population during the feast. Lodging would have been impossible to find, so Bethany was the perfect place. Had Jesus gone into Jerusalem He might have found no door open to Him. Perhaps the rejection and lack of accommodations at Bethlehem thirty-three years earlier had been enough for one lifetime.

Martha, Mary, and Lazarus had been friends with Jesus for years. The comfortable nature of old friendships was just what Jesus needed. He knew what lay in store for Him in Jerusalem. Good Friday would not catch Him by surprise. For a little while He needed the sustaining power of a good meal and old friends. I am sure the memory of Lazarus's death and subsequent raising by Jesus was fresh in everyone's mind. News had spread that the miracle worker was in Bethany, and many wanted to see Him. The pressure Jesus felt must have been tremendous.

On Sunday Jesus joined the crowds heading into Jerusalem. Others gathered along the road when they heard that the Galilean prophet was coming. James Stewart described the scene this way:

> Great companies of pilgrims were flocking in toward the city; and others, hearing that the Galilean prophet, whose fame was now nation-wide, was approaching, came out to line the roads and watch him as he passed. All reserve was now over; and when Jesus entered Jerusalem on that Palm Sunday, he entered it as God's Messiah. That was the meaning of the pageantry of that tumultuous hour, and he openly accepted the tribute. Popularity had waxed and waned, but now for a brief moment it was reborn. Suddenly the flame that had died to a cold ember blazed up again. Most of the pilgrims who acclaimed Jesus with their hosannas were no doubt provincials, his own countrymen from Galilee in the north—an entirely different crowd from the city rabble which was to cry "Crucify him," before the week was over.[1]

Many people had turned their backs on Jesus by that time, but many others still followed Him and believed He was someone special. Jesus was willing for them to do so. At the beginning of His ministry, He avoided recognition and what we today would call publicity. By the time He rode into Jerusalem, however, He was ready to be known for His genuine identity.

Jesus was welcomed as a triumphant King. The people wanted Him to be the kind of conquering hero spoken of in some of their contemporary poetry of militant nationalism. Part of one such poem says:

> Behold, O Lord, and raise up their king, the son
> of David,
>   at the time thou hast appointed, O God,
>   to reign over Israel thy servant.
> Gird him with strength to shatter wicked rulers.
>   Cleanse Jerusalem from the Gentiles who
>   trample it and destroy.
> In wisdom, in justice, may he thrust out sinners
>   from God's heritage,
>   crush the arrogance of the sinner like a
>   potter's crocks,
>   crush his whole substance with an iron mace, blot
>   out the lawless Gentiles with a word, put the
>   Gentiles to flight with his threats![2]

C. H. Dodd suggested that the Jews might well have substituted the word *Romans* for *Gentiles* in using this poem.

When Jesus rode into Jerusalem that Sunday, He seemed to many people the perfect image of the conquering hero come to drive out the hated Romans and set up His own throne. The people shouted at His approach, "Blessed is he who comes in the name of the Lord!" and "Blessed is the coming kingdom of our father David!" and "Hosanna in the highest!" (Mark 11:9-10). The people who lined the road felt that finally someone was going to *do* something instead of just talk. Of course, they already had some who wanted to do things. There were plenty of leaders of insurrections and revolts. One was in prison in Jerusalem. He was called Barabbas. This man's first name was Jesus too. His last name is from two words: *bar,* meaning "son of," and *abba,"* meaning "father." His name was Jesus, son of the father, and he waited in a Roman prison while Jesus, Son of the Father, rode into town to proclaim His coming kingdom.

The entry was like Mardi Gras in New Orleans. The shouts of praise, the waving of palm branches, and the soaring hopes of the people—all affected Jesus deeply, but not in the way the crowds expected Jesus did not take on the role they wanted to give Him. Luke says that when Jesus arrived at the outskirts of Jerusalem He did something almost unbelievable—He cried. With deep sadness, He said through his tears, "If you, even you, had only known on this day what would bring you peace—but now it is hidden from your eyes." With deep pathos Jesus felt the strain of the sight before Him. It must have been a double feeling, a feeling on one hand of excitement and anticipation and on the other of distress and sorrow. He was a good citizen of His nation, and its impending doom broke His heart. But Jesus was God's representative, too, and He could never be hemmed in by national boundaries and geographical limits. All the earth was His—Rome as well as Galilee. The sight of that old city, with its centuries of history and tradition, seemed to reach into the very heart of Christ. Deeply moved, He could not hold back the tears. And why should He? Crying is not unmanly.

He wept for the people because they were so blind. The crowd wanted a military leader—a conquering hero—but Jesus brought no swinging sword or charging cavalry. He brought only Himself and His authoritative word. If His kingdom were to come, that would have to be enough.

Jesus made His entry into the city with the knowledge that whatever happened, that journey was necessary.

Events were coming to a head. An irresistible force was about to meet an immovable object. Jesus knew that His life was in jeopardy, but His life was not for hoarding or protecting. Had He not said, "Whoever wants to save his life will lose it, but whoever loses his life for me will save it"?

Jesus' journey of faith was like an old legend of a Jew who lived in Krakow, Poland. One night the Jew had a vivid dream about the city of Prague and of a certain bridge with treasure buried beneath it. This man's name was Simon, son of Jacob. Simon was poor, so the dream excited him greatly. He dreamed the same dream several nights in a row. It was so real that Simon decided he must travel to Prague to see if he could find the treasure. One morning he got up very early and began his long journey to Prague. When he finally arrived, he knew where to go because the city was just like his dream. Simon went immediately to the bridge and began looking for the treasure.

As he was searching, a policeman grabbed him and demanded to know what he was doing. Simon patiently explained his vivid dream and the long journey to Prague. The policeman laughed and said, "You foolish old man. Don't you know that you can't believe dreams? Why, I myself have been dreaming of a certain Simon, son of Jacob, who lives in Krakow. In the dream he has a fabulous treasure buried under the stove in his kitchen. But do I go running off to Krakow looking for someone who might not even exist? Or there might be hundreds of Simons, sons of Jacob. Now, old man, get out of here!" Simon went back to Krakow, looked under the stove in his kitchen, found the treasure, and lived comfortably for the rest of his life.[3] The rabbis who used to tell this story would add this ending: The treasure was always in Krakow, but the knowledge of the treasure was in Prague.

In going into Jerusalem as He did, Jesus made that kind

of journey of faith. Ringing in his mind were the words of the prophet Zechariah who said:

> Rejoice greatly, O Daughter of Zion!
>   Shout, daughter of Jerusalem!
> See, your king comes to you,
>   righteous and having salvation,
>   gentle and riding on a donkey,
>   on a colt, the foal of a donkey (9:9).

That was a far cry from the conquering general who would sweep into Jerusalem in a chariot pulled by two white horses. Perhaps the tears Jesus shed at the city's outskirts gave the people a hint that His idea of His task was very different from their idea. They wanted a Jewish general. Jesus gave them someone they could neither compare to anyone else, nor could they fully comprehend Him. Jesus was what William Barclay called the "Knight of Bethlehem":

> There was a Knight of Bethlehem,
>   Whose wealth was tears and sorrows,
> His men-at-arms were little lambs,
>   His trumpeters were sparrows.
> His castle was a wooden Cross
>   On which He hung so high;
> His helmet was a crown of thorns,
>   Whose crest did touch the sky.[4]

Jesus' view of His work went against every common notion of power. It still does. We usually think in terms of "power over," some sort of authority or force with which we can make people do what we want them to do. Jesus demonstrated the concept of "power with," a collaboration of wills to accomplish His good. The difference between "power over" and "power with" is enormous. Henri Nouwen spoke of the former when he observed,

One of the greatest ironies of the history of Christianity is that its leaders constantly gave in to the temptation of power—political power, military power, economic power, or moral and spiritual power—even though they continued to speak in the name of Jesus, who did not cling to his divine power but emptied himself and became as we are. The temptation to consider power an apt instrument for the proclamation of the Gospel is the greatest of all."[5]

Nouwen pointed out that this temptation to power is so great because it offers an easy substitute for the hard task of love: "It seems easier to be God than to love God, easier to control people than to love people, easier to own life than to love life."

On the night of His arrest, Jesus had to resist this temptation and to rebuke Simon Peter for giving in to it. When the crowd came to Gethsemane to take Jesus away, Peter pulled a sword and whacked off an ear of the high priest's servant. Jesus said to him, "Put your sword back in its place, . . . for all who draw the sword will die by the sword. Do you think I cannot call on my Father, and he will at once put at my disposal more than twelve legions of angels?" (Matt. 26:52-53). The way of the sword has never been the way of Christ, twenty centuries of crusades, inquisitions, slavery, corruption, and the manipulation of consciences not withstanding!

Jesus' entry into Jerusalem was the responsible thing for Him to do. That is one fact that stands out so clearly in the Gospels. He knew what was in store for Him in the city, but He went anyway. An arrest warrant had already been issued for Him. The Talmud, a commentary on the Jewish law, was written over a seven-century period, from about 200 B.C. to A.D. 500. It spells out an indictment against one Heshu Hannosri. Some scholars believe this was the Hebrew name for Jesus of Nazareth:

Wanted: Heshu Hannosri
   He shall be stoned because he has practiced sorcery and
enticed Israel to apostasy. Anyone who can say anything in
his favor, let him come forward and plead on his behalf.
Anyone who knows where he is, let him declare it to the
Great Sanhedrin in Jerusalem.

Even with that inditement hanging over Him, Jesus always
acted responsibly. That fact causes me to draw nearer to
Him and admire Jesus even more. I get angry at irresponsi-
bility, especially when it is of a selfish and perverted sort.
Most of us are repulsed by gross negligence. We see some
neglect or dereliction of duty and wonder, *How did that ever
happen?* Consider these examples of seemingly insane
behavior.
   A man in New York City was depressed and wanted to
commit suicide. He jumped into the path of a subway train.
Instead of being killed the man was badly injured. He
promptly sued the New York subway authority and collect-
ed $650,000 in damages!
   A man was attempting to rob a school was on the roof,
looking for a way to get into the building. He fell through
a skylight and then sued the educational district. The insurance company was required to pay the would-be robber
$260,000 plus $1,500 per month for several years!
   Two neighbors had a hedge which separated their
houses. The two neighbors held a lawn mower over the
hedge to trim it. The mower slipped in their hands and cut
two fingers off one of the men. He sued the store which sold
him the mower for not telling him that the lawn mower was
not a hedge trimmer, and he won. The store's insurance
company had to settle financially.
   An overweight man with a heart condition bought a lawn
mower. When he tried to start it, he had a heart attack. He
was awarded $1,800,000 in damages!
   A man making a call from a phone booth in California

was hit by a drunken driver who crashed over the sidewalk and struck the booth. The state supreme court held the designers of the phone booth responsible!

A woman in California gave birth to seven infants which were twelve weeks premature. One was stillborn, and three others died. Even though the remaining three babies weighed less than two pounds at birth, the medical staff worked to save them and eventually succeeded. The parents took their three infants home and filed a $2.2 million suit against the doctor and clinic that had administered fertility drugs to the mother!

A woman in Minnesota gave birth to a child affected with Downs Syndrome. She sued her obstetrician for not recommending amniocentesis and abortion. A judge in the case awarded her damages for "wrongful birth"![6]

My blood boils when I hear of things like that. Life in general is a risk, and it cannot be fully insured. And I know of no insurance against stupidity. A what's-in-it-for-me attitude is deadly for both individuals and a nation. Jesus would have none of this. He acted responsibily all His life. At age twelve He was responsible to the active questioning and probing in His own mind. On a trip to Jerusalem for the Feast of Passover, Jesus became so involved with the discussions of religious matters His parents left without Him, and He did not seem to notice. There were other pressing matters, issues which were above the claims of even His family. Because He was responsible to these matters at even a young age, Jesus "grew in wisdom and statute, and in favor with God and men" (Luke 2:52).

Jesus was responsible in refusing some things. The desert temptations show that in order for Him to find His way He had first to reject the way of others. Satan offered easy success, short-lived popularity, and manipulative power. To these Jesus said no.

Jesus was responsible in accepting some things. He accepted baptism by John as a sign of solidarity with His people. He accepted the limitations of the human condition during His incarnation. Jesus accepted the changeable nature of the crowd which hailed Him one day but reviled Him afterwards. Edwin McNeill Poteat has spoken of this change in the poem, "Palm Sunday and Monday":

> They pluck their palm branches and hail Him as King,
>   Early on Sunday;
> They spread their garments; hosannas they sing,
>   Early on Sunday.
> But where is the noise of their hurrying feet,
>   The crown they would offer, the sceptre, the seat?
> Their King wanders hungry, forgot in the street,
>   Early on Monday.[7]

He even accepted a cross that was thrust upon Him several days later. That cross became a sign for everyone, even if it means different things to different people. Herschel H. Hobbs said of the cross:

> How varied are the views men have of the Cross! To many, it is but an ornament to be worn about the neck. To the architect it is a symbol, adorning churches. To the scholar it is a goad, driving him on in intellectual pursuits. To the preacher it is a sermon, filling the need of the hour—and of eternity. To the skeptic it is a superstition, clouding men's souls. . . . To Christ it was a bier and a throne, paradox of time, predestined to eternity. To multiplied millions of storm-tossed souls it is an anchor, offering a haven of rest.[8]

Whatever it might have become, Jesus accepted it with full responsibility. Have you noticed that what we call the "seven last words" from the cross were all statements of responsibility? He said, "Father, forgive them for they do not know what they are doing." It was a responsible word for the needs of the ignorant. Jesus said to His mother, "Dear woman, here is your son," and to one disciple, "Here is your mother." It was a responsible word for the care of Mary. He called out, "I am thirsty." It was a responsible word for His bodily needs. Jesus told one man on the cross, "I tell you the truth, today you will be with me in paradise." This was a responsible word for His brother's need. He cried out, "My God, why have you forsaken me?" It was a responsible word of His heart's need. Jesus whispered, "Father, into your hands I commit my spirit." It was a responsible word for His soul's need. Finally, He breathed, "It is finished." It was a responsible word for the world's need.

Jesus was responsible in telling the truth and living the truth. His entry into Jerusalem was an "acted parable."9 It was a sign, but only those with open minds could understand the symbolism of the donkey rather than a charging stallion. His conquering would be done on the battlefields of the mind and not in the streets of Jerusalem. His victory would last for eternity instead of falling with the century.

Hearing the Word Today

On the surface appearance, Jesus' journey into Jerusalem was disastrous. The week began with adoration that was followed by rejection, then humiliation, and finally crucifixion. It makes little sense in the normal meaning of that word. From God's perspective, however, it was absolutely necessary.

Carl Sandburg wrote a multivolume set of books on the life of Abraham Lincoln. One volume has a chapter entitled "Palm Sunday '65." It was about the date of April 9, 1865 when Robert E. Lee surrendered to Ulysses S. Grant at Appomattox Court House in Virginia. On that Palm Sunday, the war ended and peace began to reign. A few skirmishes flared up here and there until everyone finally got the word, but the war really was over. That is not a bad analogy to what happened on the day of Jesus' last ride into

Jerusalem. God was ready to present His peace plan to humanity. There would be no compromise. A skirmish broke out on Friday, but people did not yet realize that the battle was over.

Palm Sunday is the day when Christ proclaimed His victory over the hostile forces opposed to Him. He faced these forces armed only with power of self-giving love, but that was enough. God is still seeking to let everyone know the battle is over and that Christ won. Jesus' life itself was the treaty.

Notes

1. James S. Stewart, *The Life and Teaching of Jesus Christ* (New York: Abingdon Press, n.d.), 145-146.

2. From the so-called Psalms of Solomon, 17:23-27. This passage is given in C. H. Dodd, *The Founder of Christianity* (New York: Macmillan Publishing Co., 1970), 143.

3. This story is told by Belden C. Lane in a series of lectures on the use of stories in theology, *Storytelling: the Enchantment of Theology* (Four cassette tapes: St. Louis: Bethany Press, 1981).

4. William Barclay, *The Gospel of Luke*, The Daily Study Bible (Edinburgh: Saint Andrew University Press, 1957, 3rd ed.), 174.

5. Henri J. M. Nouwen, *In the Name of Jesus* (New York: The Crossroad Publishing Co., 1989), 58.

6. These cases are related by Dr. James Dobson in his "Focus on the Family" newsletter dated 24 February 1986.

7. From Charles L. Wallis, ed., *Worship Resources for Special Days* (Grand Rapids: Baker Book House, 1976 [reprint of the 1954 ed.]), 65.

8. Herschel H. Hobbs, quoted in ibid., 94-95.

9. Stewart, 146.

2

MONDAY

Exposing Barren Lives

We can now understand that the fate of the soul is the fate of the social order, that if the spirit within us withers, so too will all the world we build about us.   —Theodore Roszak

Anger and cursing are generally not associated with righteous causes. Flaring tempers and words that would blister the paint off the walls are usually thought of as vices of "bad" people. On the final Monday of Jesus' life, He had occasion to express His anger and to use a curse for holy purposes. The incidents make us pause and ask, "What is going on here?" Mark 11 contains two of the most puzzling episodes in Jesus' entire life. One is the cleansing of the Temple, and the other is the cursing of a fig tree. These two stories are unusual because they both seem out of character for Jesus.

In the first, He made a whip out of chords and drove out the money changers. That has caused Christians for two thousand years to scratch their heads and wonder about Christ's anger. After all, wasn't this the same man who said, "Love your enemies"? How do you square that statement against the sting of a whip?

The second story here is just as oblique, if not more so. Jesus' stomach growled on that last Monday of His life, and He wanted a meal. He spotted a fig tree in the distance as He headed toward Jerusalem, so He lead His disciples over to that spot. Instead of figs, however, Jesus found only leaves. Then He said those words which have troubled people for years: "May no one ever eat fruit from you again." Simon Peter called those words a curse (Mark 11: 21). Were these two events occasions when Jesus' anger got the best of Him and when He swore at a helpless fig tree? Let us look a bit deeper into this account.

Mark's Gospel ties these two stories closely together. For Mark the cleansing of the Temple and the cursing of the fig tree were the twin lanes of the same road. Both together served as Jesus' teaching tool as He instructed His followers on that fateful Monday morning.

Cleansing the Temple

Evil that masquerades as good is the most stubborn, difficult, and slippery form of evil. We have trouble with this sort of evil because it is like a spy—it hides pretending to do one thing while it actually accomplishes something else. How, for example, did an obscure former convict become the chancellor of Germany in the 1930s? He promised his people that he would elevate them from their humiliating defeat of World War I. Hitler regarded himself as something of a "savior" of his nation. He seemed on the surface to be a good, helpful man. The result of his subterfuge was, of course, World War II.

Jesus ran up against that sort of evil. On the last Monday of Jesus' life, He took on the task of cleansing the Temple in Jerusalem. Mark tells us that Jesus had entered that city on what we call Palm Sunday. "He looked around at everything, but since it was already late, he went out to Bethany with the Twelve" (11:11). The next morning he came back into town. Jesus saw the fig tree along the road, was disappointed with the yield, and pronounced a curse upon the tree. The fig tree with no fruit and the Temple with no fruit were virtually the same thing in Jesus' eyes.

The Temple system Jesus' day seems to have been a mixture of religion, power, and commerce. This was an explosive mixture, even as it is today. Recent scandals involving television evangelists testify to this fact. The Jewish people were obligated to pay a yearly Temple tax.[1] That tax was due in the month of Adar, the month which came immediately before the month of Nisan in which Passover occurred. That tax was about the equivalent of two days' pay. Exactly one month before Passover, stalls were erected in all the towns and villages so people could pay this tax. They stayed open until the twenty-fifth day of Adar. After that date the tax could be paid only in the Temple in Jerusalem.

Scholars note that the Temple was constructed in a series of courts. The outer court was called the court of the Gentiles. Persons of any race, gender, or nationality could enter there. Beyond that and closer to the center was the court of the women. Next came the court of the Israelites. Men who came to sacrifice entered there and handed the sacrifices to the priests at a rail in this court. The court of the priests was next. The priests entered there and offered the sacrifices upon an alter of the burnt offerings. The sellers of the animals in the Temple area offered animals for these sacrifices. A person could buy one there rather than bring one of his own. It was a matter of convenience for the purchaser as much as the purity of the sacrificial animal.

The final inner court was the holy place which was the Temple proper. At the west end of this, behind a veil, was the holy of holies, the place considered most sacred. The high priest entered there only once a year on the Day of Atonement. There he offered sacrifices for the sins of the entire nation.

By the time of Jesus, the outer court, the court of the Gentiles, had become more of a circus or zoo than a place of worship. One scholar said it was "an oriental bazaar, making it impossible for any Gentile to use the area for prayer or serious devotion to God."[2] If you have ever been to a modern auction barn, you might have an idea of what it was like. How could a person worship on a carnival midway? The poor Jews and Gentiles, for whom this area supposedly existed, were fleeced out of their hard-earned cash but had great trouble focusing on worship.

The religious pilgrims who went to the Temple wanted to offer animals for sacrifice or thanksgiving. They could have brought animals from home for this purpose, but there was a catch. The Temple authorities had their staff of "inspectors" on duty. Their function was to examine every animal for sacrifice in order to ensure it met the specification of being unblemished. If an animal were brought in from the outside, the person bringing it had to pay a small fee for it to be inspected. The inspector was almost certain to find some flaw in the animal. If the animal was bought inside the Temple, however, the animal was already inspected and guaranteed clean. The animals sold inside the Temple cost about 40 percent more than ones on the outside. Thus, the Temple authorities had a stranglehold on the "business" of sacrifice.

In addition to animal sellers, the court of the Gentiles also had moneychangers. They were necessary because the Temple tax had to be paid in certain kinds of currency—either half shekels or in Galilean shekels. Other currency was not accepted because the heads of various kings was engraved on it. Such graven images were unclean for the purposes of worship. The money changers accepted any sort of currency and exchange it for the "clean" money which was accepted in the Temple.

Pilgrims were, thus, in a double bind. First they were forced to pay the Temple tax, and second, they were forced to use only certain kinds of currency. The money changers imposed a surcharge on the transaction of as much as 12 percent. This can still be a racket. I once took a trip to England and exchanged American money for British currency at Kennedy Airport. I learned later that I could have gotten much better rates had I waited until I got to London and then made the transaction at a bank. A scholar well acquainted with the time in question has said, "What was little better than a gigantic financial swindle was being worked on poor pilgrims who could ill afford it. The matter was often complicated by the fact that the silver of the coins offered was worn and the coins were thin; they were then weighed, and there was further grasping and acrimonious dispute as to their true value."[3]

This, then, was the scene when Jesus lived. The Temple should have been a place of peace and tranquility that had an aura conducive to worship. Instead it was of place of noise as the traders and pilgrims haggled, swore, and bargained for animals and coins. What should have been a place filled with the fragrance of the knowledge of God (see 2 Cor. 2:14) was filled with the smell of sheep dung and pigeon droppings. The place that should have been open and inviting was closed and costly. William Barclay has noted:

> Many must have come to the Temple with a sense of hope that perhaps there they might find God; and instead they found a swaying, disputing, bargaining mob, and an atmosphere in which devotion was impossible. The place which should have been, as Mark put it, a house of prayer "for all nations" had become a market place where avaricious traders swindled and shrewd tourists bargained. There are other ways than that of producing an atmosphere within a church in which it is very difficult for the simple seeker to find God, and any who render the search for God more difficult must face the anger of Jesus.[4]

Jesus was angry—good and angry. He should have been!

How could anyone with any moral sensibilities view the Temple with its corruption and *not* be angry? Many modern Christians have great difficulty with anger. We have been taught that to be angry is wrong. Certainly, harboring strong feelings of hostility is wrong. If I am hostile toward my brother, my hostility hurts me much more than it hurts him. Our responsibility is to deal with the feelings and not let them smoulder like coals that will burst into flame at many moment. Paul said, for example. "Therefore each of you must put off falsehood and speak truthfully to his neighbor, for we are all members of one body. 'In your anger do not sin': Do not let the sun go down while you are still angry, and do not give the devil a foothold" (Eph. 4:25-27). The phrase "put off falsehood" means among other things that we are to be honest in our feelings, including anger.

One expert in the area of anger management has noted that the twentieth century has fostered an impoverished stewardship of anger in two ways:

> (1) We have persisted in preaching and pretending that all anger is sin and that when present it is best disguised; (2) we have most often acted out the illusion that hard feelings are best left alone, unexamined and untouched, as if that actually was a superior solution to the biblical injunction that we ought to face up to our differences with others (Matt. 18:15 *ff*). What we need to risk and believe is that there are creative Christian ways to handle our deepest feelings directly without being overwhelmed or overwhelming in our message.[5]

These deep feelings of anger, if they are held in long enough, can produce an "anesthesia of feelings" which can lead to general apathy.[6]

Whatever else might be said of Jesus, He had no apathy, nor did He hold in His strong feelings. He was a good steward of His anger. Instead of allowing it to harm Him, He used it as a righteous tool in clearing the money changers and animal sellers out of the Temple. John's Gospel says that Jesus made a whip out of chords and drove out both the animals and the people. Jesus protested the crass commercialism which used legitimate religious feelings to squeeze money out of people who felt the deep need to worship God. He also protested the effective closing off of the Temple to the Gentiles.

As he flailed the whip and flipped over the tables, Jesus quoted two passages from the Old Testament. The first is from Isaiah 56:7 which reads in its entirety:

> "These I will bring to my holy mountain
>   and give them joy in my house of prayer
> Their burnt offerings and sacrifices
>   will be accepted on my altar;
> for my house will be called
>   a house of prayer for all nations."

The trouble was that the Temple was no longer a worship place for all people. It was for the Jews. They had excluded others by making them stay out in the far courtyards. How could a Gentile worship when he was kept in the outer areas where the buying and selling and haggling over coins was going on? "For all nations," Jesus had said. "For Israel only," the Jews had said.

The second passage Jesus quoted was from Jeremiah 7:11: "Has this house, which bears my Name, become a den of robbers to you? But I have been watching! declares the Lord." The swindlers and chiselers had set up shop in God's house and were effectively robbing religious pilgrims.

Another thing the people were doing was using the Temple as a shortcut through the city. In Mark 11:16 we read that Jesus would not allow anyone to carry merchandise through the Temple courts.

The place which should have been a holy, open, inviting place had been turned into a secular, exclusive, convenient shop for fleecing the gullible and cashing in on deep religious feelings. Jesus was furious! Thank God! There has always been room in God's work for the prophet who sees with a clear eye and speaks with a right tongue. Amos thundered against the absurdity of his nation's leaders. Jeremiah warned about foreign intrigue. There are those even today who are always ready to speak up for the poor and leftout.[7] It was Jesus, though, who lifted the prophetic word and act to a new level.

Cursing the Fig Tree

The account of the withered fig tree seems strange to contemporary readers whose sensitivities are shocked at Jesus' actions. Even in the Scriptures themselves this story seems unusual. Matthew shortened the story, and Luke omitted it completely. Mark gave the fullest account. On what we call Palm Sunday, Jesus entered Jerusalem but then went back to Bethany to spend the night. The next morning, on Monday, He and the disciples were on their way back to Jerusalem when Jesus spotted a fig tree in full leaf. He went up to it expecting to find it full of fruit. He found nothing, however. Mark 11:14 says, "Then he said to the tree, 'May no one ever eat fruit from you again.' And his disciples heard him say it." The next day, Tuesday morning, Jesus and the twelve were again going to Jerusalem. They saw that the tree had withered overnight. Simon Peter said, "Rabbi, look! The fig tree you cursed has withered!" This story causes some modern people trouble because of a misunderstanding of the concept of curse in the Bible. A biblical curse was not what we today would call a "four-letter word." It was not "nasty" or a scatological reference. A good Oriental curse was earthy, specific, and a call to action. It might be something like these two: "May the fleas of a thousand camels infest your armpits," and "May all your teeth fall out but one, and in that one may you get a toothache." In cursing the fig tree, Jesus was calling for action on the part of His disciples and using it as an object lesson or prophetic symbolism.

This story was tied by Mark to the cleansing of the Temple. A fig tree with no fruit was exactly like a Temple which produced no fruit. One commentator noted:

> The incident of the fig tree both interprets the cleansing of
> the Temple and is interpreted by the latter incident. Jesus'
> disappointment with the fig tree is like his disappointment
> with Israel and the temple, her chief shrine. His judgment
> pronounced upon the tree is like the threat of God's judg-
> ment soon to fall upon the city of Jerusalem.[8]

The cursing of the tree was a prophetic sign. Isaiah had gone naked to show what would happen to the nation (Isa. 20:1-6). Jeremiah smashed a clay pot to symbolize the fate of his nation (Jer. 19:1-13). Ezekiel drew on a clay tablet a city under siege. It was a symbol of the coming siege of Jerusalem (Ezek. 4:1-17).[9] Jesus did not swear at the tree but rather used it as an object lesson for His disciples.

The fig tree's leaves promised fruit, but there was no fruit. The tree's appearance was deceptive. It was a symbol of what Jesus had found in the Temple. It, too, looked promising. The Temple had a long history and promised seekers that they would find a place of worship, a place that would help them find God. What they found was chaos like the day after Christmas at a department store. To this farce Jesus raised His whip and His voice and said in effect, "Enough! You shall not make my Father's House a place of empty promises in which you are more interested in revenue than reverence."

What fruit was Jesus seeking? We get a clue in the rest of the story in Mark 11:22-26. When Simon Peter pointed out that the fig tree had withered, Jesus moved immediately into teaching His disciples about two fruit which should grow out of a vibrant life. One is faith. "Have faith in God," He told Simon. It is the sort of faith that can make a mountain move from its foundation and jump into the ocean. The other fruit is forgiveness. "And when you stand praying, if you hold anything against anyone, forgive him, so that your Father in heaven may forgive you your sins." These were the very things Jesus found lacking in the Temple. It should have been an instrument to foster faith and encourage forgiveness. A bad religion or institution is thus all leaf and no fruit, all show and no substance.

Hearing the Word Today

When any religious institution or individual is more interested in survival and comfort than in worship and service, watch out! I personally am not swayed by people who only talk about faith and ethics. I am swayed by people who are ethical and who are faithful. Emily Dickinson protested in one of her poems against one who was all talk:

> He preached upon "breadth" till it argued him narrow—
> The broad are too broad to define;
> And of "Truth" until it proclaimed him a Liar—
> The Truth never flaunted a Sign—
> Simplicity fled from this counterfeit presence
> As Gold the Pyrites would shun—
> What confusion would cover the innocent Jesus
> To meet so enabled a Man!

The Temple in Jesus' day did not go from genuine devotion to commercialism overnight. The changes occurred gradually. Such changes usually do. I doubt that certain religious leaders who have lost their influence did so overnight. They did not simply wake up one day and decide, "Well, I'm bored with my life. I think I'll do something drastic to add a little excitement." Instead, their fall was bit by bit over a long time. The effects of their actions may have surfaced in a short time, but the decision to do certain things came about over time. Paul Scherer has written of this sort of downward, gradual movement:

> There is much that may be quite crude and overt, but much that may be so unbelievably subtle as for years to go unnoticed, about the process by which a holy place is profaned, turned into a bargain counter where peace of mind and health of body and very heaven itself are marked down at cut rates—formerly a cross, now a trinket—and God is blasphemed (Rom. 2:24). Any distortion, inevitably moving toward perversion, of the true purpose for which the church exists; every secularization of her life; her prostitution to the economic order or to the state; such manipulation of her message or of her ministry as to make either of them a means to some end beyond itself (Mark 11:16); the corruption of her fellowship by class consciousness, by race discrimination, by privilege, by pride of virtue or of doctrine, self-righteous and exclusive—what is it but to change "the truth of God into a lie," to worship and serve "the creature more than the Creator, who is blessed for ever" (Rom. 1:25)?[10]

The Temple had everything needed to be, as Jesus Himself had said, "a house of prayer for all nations." But the Jews interpreted God's election of them as a privilege rather than a responsibility. It became a place to be cursed by those hurt by it, and a place to be avoided, if possible. How much is that like some churches? As far as I can tell, God does not save people because they deserve it but because they need it. We have no right to group together in exclusive churches of fortress mentality which say by attitude if not action: "This is *our* church. Let's just see you try to get into here!" How many churches have signs which proclaim, "Everybody welcome" but which would have a collective heart attack if the "wrong kind" of people tried to attend?

A British theologian Harry Blamires argued that there is no subtler perversion of Christianity than to treat it as merely a means to worldly ends. He said, "The Christian Faith is important because it is true. What it happens to achieve, in ourselves or in others, is another, and strictly speaking, secondary matter." Blamires further noted, "What a mean blasphemy it would be, to go through magnificent acts of public worship always with the dominant intention at the back of the mind—'This is really going to make a better chap of me!' What arrogance and presumption, to treat eternal God, throned in glory, as a visual aid to moral self-improvement."[11] Worship *does* help. Faith *does* help. Faith *does* make us better people. But the reason for worship is not primarily *our* betterment or *our* self-congratulations. It is for *God.* This is what the men in charge of the Temple in Jesus' day forgot.

This is precisely why the church today is not a religious institution. The church does not exist so people can be religious and do religious kinds of things. The church exists as a means to focus upon God in worship and as a channel to introduce people to the Lord. We do not gather in our churches for merely private, introverted, self-seeking goals. Faith may, indeed, make us more lovable to our families, but Christ did not die to make us more lovable. Being a member of a church might help us deal with daily frustrations, but Jesus did not lay down His life in order to be resurrected as some primordial psychologist.

The focus of the church today is not on precise religious duties which are legalistic and restrictive. Christ came to offer us the abundant life of freedom in the Spirit, not the guilt-ridden life which continually drags some religious ball and chain. Jesus once scolded the Pharisees for being meticulous about straining out gnats but swallowing camels (Matt. 23:24). They so focused on trivial matters that they missed the important stuff. Legalism does not work.

Ours is very much an age of image and status. People seem more concerned with the way they appear on the outside than with what they are on the inside. I recently saw an ad in a newspaper for a car phone antenna. It did not work and could not be hooked up to anything. You were just supposed to buy it, place it on your car, and let people think you had a car phone. (Why not add wings and let them think you have your own private jet?)

A Temple teeming with hucksters and a withered fig tree stand as stark symbols that God is not to be trifled with. The lives of the leaders of the Temple were as barren as the tree outside Jerusalem. Jesus exposed those barren lives and then laid down His life that they, and we, might find reality, substance, genuine life. Lee Iacocca once gave a speech in which he referred to the Statue of Liberty: "If Miss Liberty was a symbol of hope, Ellis Island was a symbol of reality. We need both of these symbols because our country is not based on hope alone, but on sweat and pain."[12] In a like manner, the Temple was a symbol of devotion, but the fig tree stands for the impossibility of ignoring responsibility. Both stand together as God's invitation to worship but also His warning about being fruitful.

Seen any fig trees lately?

Notes

1. Information on the Temple tax and manner of payment is from William Barclay, *The Mind of Jesus* (New York: Harper & Row, 1960), 188-192.

2. Larry W. Hurtado, *Mark*, a Good News Commentary (New York: Harper & Row, 1983), 169.

3. Barclay, 189.

4. Ibid., 191-192.

5. Daniel B. Bagby, *Understanding Anger in the Church* (Nashville: Broadman Press, 1979), 26-27.

6. Ibid., 23. For more on apathy see, Don M. Aycock, ed., *Apathy In the Pew: Ministering to the Uninvolved* (South Plainfield, N.J.: Bridge Publishing, 1988).

7. I consider Will Campbell one such person. See Thomas L. Connelly, *Will Campbell and the Soul of the South* (New York: Continuum, 1982).

8. Hurtado, 168.

9. For more on symbolism see my article, "Preaching on Old Testament Symbols," *Proclaim*, January-March, 1988, 18-21, and my book, *Symbols of Salvation* (Nashville: Broadman Press, 1982).

10. Paul Scherer, *The Interpreter's Bible* (New York: Abingdon Press, 1952), 8:343.

11. Harry Blamires, *The Christian Mind* (London: S.P.C.K, 1963), 110.

12. Lee Iacocca, quoted in *Campbell's Notebook*. 5, 4:2.

3

TUESDAY

Exercising Authority

We, the unwilling, led by the unknowing, are doing the impossible for the ungrateful. We have done so much for so long with so little we are now qualified to do anything with nothing —Sign in a glass shop

That sign in the glass shop caught my eye. Many had stood at that spot and laughed at the nonsense, but like much humor, it has a point.[1] It prompted me to ask some questions. Why do we do what we do? Why try to help people who are ungrateful and unwilling to help themselves? Answering these questions with "We do it for the money" is not enough. The "why" and the "how" are theological questions as much as economic questions. We know it is true today, and Jesus knew this to be true.

On Tuesday of the last week of His life, Jesus went back into Jerusalem and taught in the courts of the Temple which He had cleansed the day before. We are not told if the money changers and animal sellers were back already, but I suspect they were. While Jesus was teaching, a delegation from the chief priests arrived to question Him. They asked two questions: "By what authority are you doing— these things?" (chasing the money changers out of the Temple), and "Who gave you this authority?" (RSV) The people who questioned Jesus were "the chief priests, the teachers of the law and the elders" (Mark 11:27). They were of the traditional divisions of the Sanhedrin. This body was a council of seventy-one members, appointed from the leading priests, heads of prominent Sadducean families, and from eminent pharisaic scholars. Together they formed something of a final court of appeal for the Jews in Judea. They were outraged that Jesus would be bold enough to clear the Temple without consulting them. For them the matter was fairly simple. Their power and prestige had been challenged, and they were not going to take it sitting still.

The Sanhedrin deliberated on their dilemma. They could not ignore this preacher from Nazareth because He was so popular with the people. Nor could they take effective action against Him for the same reason. One alternative they did not consider—"it did not occur to them to give him their support."[2] Playing "what if?" is always difficult, but we cannot help but wonder what might have happened if they had supported Him. In any case, they demanded His credentials. Jesus had infringed upon their privileges and power, and power never gives itself away. Power and privilege always hold onto their position until forced by a greater power to give it up. The only exception to this rule was stated by Paul in a reference to Christ in Philippians 2:6-8:

> Who, being in very nature God,
> > did not consider equality with God
> > > something to be grasped,
> but made himself nothing,
> > taking the very nature of a servant,
> > being made in human likeness.
> And being found in appearance as a man,
> > he humbled himself
> > and became obedient to death—
> > even death on a cross!

A Different Kind of Authority

From the beginning of His public ministry, Jesus had done things differently. At the beginning of Mark's Gospel, Jesus taught and drove an evil spirit out of a man. Mark noted, "The people were amazed at his teaching, because he taught them as one who had authority, not as the teachers of the law" (1:22). After Jesus drove the spirit from the man the people responded, "What is this? A new teaching —and with authority! He even gives orders to evil spirits and they obey him" (1:27). The term *authority* here is *exousia*. *Ex* means "out" or "out of" as in our word *exit*. *Ousia* means "essence" or "inner reality." Jesus' authority, His *exousia*, was thus His inner reality. He spoke "out of" His "essence." This was integrity and authenticity which had never been seen before or since.

In His teaching commonly called the Sermon on the Mount, Jesus reminded His hearers that they had already heard much of what He wanted to teach them. They had heard it but had not understood it or taken it seriously. He said, "Do not think that I have come to abolish the Law or the Prophets; I have not come to abolish them but to fulfill them" (Matt. 5:17). He fulfilled them in His interpretation, but more importantly, in His life. Jesus said, "You have heard that it was said . . . But I tell you." He said this six times in the fifth chapter of Matthew. In no instance did He quote another rabbi or footnote His word with other sources. Jesus simply said, "I tell you," and it was the truth. He spoke out of His essence, and His word was genuine. As one contemporary scholar noted, "For *His* understanding of God's will Jesus appeals neither to other words of Scripture nor to any tradition, but with an emphatic 'I' authoritatively sets his commands in opposition to the traditional understanding of the will of God."[3]

Other teachers and rabbis had derived authority. It came

from outside themselves and was based on citing other teachers. New interpretations of the Law was not looked upon kindly. For Jesus, though, the situation was different. His authority never consisted merely of quoting others and giving the interpretation of an authoritatively given text. Instead, "The reality of God and the authority of his will are always directly present, and are fulfilled in him."[4]

Jesus' first recorded sermon is noted in Luke 4:14-30. In His hometown of Nazareth, He went into the synagogue and read from the prophet Isaiah who said:

> "The Spirit of the Lord is on me,
>   because he has anointed me
>   to preach good news to the poor.
> He has sent me to proclaim freedom
>   for the prisoners
>   and recovery of sight for the blind,
> to release the oppressed,
>   to proclaim the year of the Lord's favor"
>   (vv. 18-19).

After reading that section, Jesus said, "Today this scripture is fulfilled in your hearing." In other words, "The one spoken of by Isaiah is standing here today." For this perceived blasphemy, the town's people became furious and tried to throw Jesus off a cliff.

The point is that Jesus felt Himself early in His ministry to possess a special kind of authority. It came from God and was evident to those who wanted to see or experience it. Not all did, however. The pattern of His life was to work with people and perform His miracles in such a way as to invite faith but never to force it. Not everyone who saw His or His disciples' power at work came to the same conclusion. The disciples who carried on missionary work after Jesus' death did some mighty works. On the day of Pentecost, for example, a miracle of communication happened in their midst. Only those who had eyes of faith could see it, however. The rest said, "They have had too much wine." It is much like Elizabeth Barrett Browning's poem which says,

> Earth's crammed with heaven,
> And every common bush afire with God;
> And only he who sees takes off his shoes—
> The rest sit round it and pluck blackberries.

Some in Jesus' day saw, and some did not. The members in the Sanhedrin who questioned Jesus on that fateful Tuesday could have seen His authority had they been open-minded. But they had already made up their minds and had set about trying to find a way to trap Jesus in His own words. "By what authority are you doing these things?" they demanded. "Who gave you authority to do this?" they wondered. It was their way of trying to slip a noose over Jesus' head, and they thought He was dumb enough to tighten the knot!

Jesus was a real human being—a *real* one. That fact always gives us trouble. I think we are less uncomfortable with His divinity than with His humanity. His answer to the Sanhedrin is classic. He answered a question—which He knew He could not answer to their satisfaction—with a question, and He also knew they could not answer to His satisfaction. His mind was very sharp and alert. They thought they were trapping Him, but they ended up being the victim of their own question.

Jesus' question to them was, on the surface, very simple: "John's baptism—was it from heaven, or from men? Tell me!" (Mark 11:30). What could they say? Mark's Gospel says that the delegation huddled to search for a response: "They discussed it among themselves and said, 'If we say, "From heaven," he will ask, "Then why didn't you believe him?" But if we say, "From men". . . . [They feared the

people, for everyone held that John really was a prophet.]
"So they answered Jesus, 'We don't know.' "

This answer was either a colossal lie or an admission of
their own spiritual blindness. The questioners were spiritu-
ally bankrupt,[5] did not want to be confronted by God's
revelation,[6] or were simply unwilling seriously and openly
to consider the source of Jesus' and John's authority.[7]
Whatever the case, Jesus clearly demonstrated that these
men who questioned Him about authority were themselves
confused about this matter. They had fashioned themselves
into a spiritual hierarchy that acted as if it had an exclusive
contract with God. Jesus' reply forced them to admit their
own incompetence as teachers who were in no position to
question His authority.

When the leaders replied that they could not answer
Jesus' question, He then said, "Neither will I tell you by
what authority I am doing these things." The message was
clear. At stake here was not the niceties of Jesus' formal
ordination and acceptance by the synagogue officials. C. H.
Dodd has noted, "The implication is that there is a kind of
authority which is self-authenticating; either you recognize
it or you don't, and if you don't there is nothing more to
be said."[8] The Pharisees *could* have seen had they wanted
to. They could have noticed what was happening around
them if they had been willing to stop interpreting every
event in terms of what it might do to their position and
prestige. They had to look and be open to the moving of
the Spirit. Jesus once used an image of an old wine skin
trying to hold new wine. The new wine was in the process
of fermenting and the expanding, pushing gases would
burst through old brittle wine skins. That was what was
happening in His life. He was bursting through every
boundary and wall which artificially separated people from
people and from God. In that regard, men and women
today are not much different from those who heard Jesus'

words first. We must be open to God's Spirit, or we cannot be convinced of His authority over us.

Jesus' authority was of this self-authenticating kind. On one occasion John the Baptist was in prison and had second thoughts about Jesus. He sent a disciple to ask His cousin, "Are you the one who was to come, or should we expect someone else?" Jesus told the messenger, "Go back and report to John what you hear and see: The blind receive sight, the lame walk, those who have leprosy are cured, the deaf hear, the dead are raised, and the good news is preached to the poor. Blessed is the man who does not fall away on account of me" (Matt. 11:2-6) Either we see it and recognize it for what it is, or we don't. If we do, we follow. If we don't, we keep searching.

God never forces Himself on anybody. When we read through the Bible, we come away impressed with the gentle way God approaches people. He never made anyone believe in Him. Faith is not a substance or a quantity that can be placed in a test tube in a scientific laboratory and scrutinized. One cannot come away with a definitive *true* or *false*. For all its benefits, the scientific method is not the way of faith. Jesus did tell John to observe and make up his mind, but this was more a matter of relationship than scientific observation. The authority by which Jesus did His work and communicated His message was not raw power but was personal relationships—His with the Father and His with those who would believe.

Bases of Authority

When all is said and done, what can we believe as true and right? What authority can we believe in to show us right from wrong? P. T. Forsyth said many years ago, "There is only one thing greater than Liberty, and that is Authority."[9] This is a very bold statement, but one which I think is vital. Contemporary American society seems adrift.

We are not sure whom or what to trust. The government has been suspect in the eye of the general public ever since the Vietnam war and the Watergate scandal. Education is not as highly respected as it once was. Even religion, which once was the citadel of authority, has taken a pounding in light of recent scandals involving greed, power, and sex. We need to get clear guidance on what to believe, but who or what can even offer the guidance? Thus, the issue of authority is vital today. A look at various types of authority might help. Many sorts of authority have arisen during the past several thousand years. Russell Dilday has given a helpful digest of some of these types.[10]

One type is *coercive authority*. This is the authority used by the state or some other party which forces its laws and inflicts punishment on those who disobey. An example of this is found in 2 Chronicles 26:16-21. King Uzziah was a powerful leader and felt he could do whatever he pleased, including desecrating the Temple of the Lord.

Another type is *delegated authority*. This is the authority granted to someone by some other hgher authority. The judges in the Old Testament, for example, had delegated authority. Ultimately it was granted to them by God.

A third type is *compelling authority*. This comes from one who is an expert in a given field and who has firsthand knowledge and experience. Einstein had this kind of authority in the field of physics, but would not have made much of an impact as an advertising spokesman for shampoo.

Persuasive authority is another type of authority. This might be called logical or mental authority. It reaches its conclusions after clear, sustained thought. It is not automatically accepted, but it has the potential of persuading others to its viewpoint. A mathematician might develop a new theory of algebraic coefficients, for example. No one else might believe it until he can persuade them to his theory by the force of his logic.

Another type is *stipulated authority*. A group of people agree in advance to accept the authority of some given standard. A church might agree to work according to *Robert's Rules of Order*, for example, or sailors agree to reckon time by Greenwich mean time.

A sixth type of authority is *functional authority*. This operates for a given period of time. If I am flying in a Boeing 747, I accept the functional authority of the pilot while in the plane, but not once I reach my destination.

Customary authority is a seventh type. This is the authority which is gained and granted over a long time. In my church field, for example, which is in a rural area, I am accorded this customary authority because I am a minister. People have pretty much agreed to grant a certain authority to any minister regardless of who he is.

The eighth kind of authority is *authentic authority*. It is self-validating, and it needs no other form of support. It is sufficient in itself. This is the kind of authority which Jesus possessed. He had others, too, but this was the most important. The members of the Sanhedrin wanted to know from whom He received the authority to cleanse the Temple and teach in its outer courts. Jesus' answer hardly satisfied them. He did not clearly state the source of His authority by saying, "Yes, it comes directly from God," or "My authority comes from my ordination as a rabbi." But they really didn't want information. They were seeking to trap Him. But as John put it, "Jesus would not entrust himself to them, for he knew all men. He did not need man's testimony about man, for he knew what was in a man" (2:24-25).

Nothing external can make us be what others want us to be. Governments can enforce laws, and even the church can make people do or say certain things. This happened, for example, during the Inquisition. In the thirteenth, four-teenth, and fifteenth centuries, the Church had a firm grip on many individuals and nations. A person whom the church thought was erring from true doctrine and practice was given a chance to "repent." A period of grace was granted, and after the person confessed his error he was usually given light penalties. By 1252 under Pope Innocent IV the rules had changed. In that year he authorized the use of torture to extract "confessions." Someone putting a red-hot iron near my face might get me to say anything, but would that make me really believe it?

Genuine religious belief must come from the inside and cannot be enforced by laws or rules from the outside. Could the rules of a monastic order, for example, prevent its members from thinking about women? A story about two priests might help us understand this issue. Tanzan and Ekido were once traveling together down a muddy road. As the rain fell, they came around a bend and met a lovely young woman dressed in a silk kimono and sash. She was unable to cross the muddy road. "Come on, girl," Tanzan said. He lifted her in his arms and carried her over the mud to the other side. Ekido said nothing until they reached their lodging for the night. Then he said to Tanzan, "We priests do not go near females, especially not young and lovely ones. It is dangerous. Why did you do that?" Tanzan replied, "Ekido, I left the girl there. Are you still carrying her?"[11]

Historical Struggles with Authority

Protestants in general and Baptists in particular have had a struggle with authority since our earliest times. Some of our spiritual ancestors began to realize that a minister's manner of dress was less important than what he believed and practiced. A pamphlet printed in England in the early seventeenth century had the following conversation be-

tween a Protestant and a Puritan who had begun throwing
off ecclesiastical authority by throwing off his vestments:

The Protestant: Well ouer-taken, Sir, whither trauel you?

The Puritane: I trauel towards the Parliament.

The Protestant: What, are you one of the *Burgesses?*

The Puritane: No, I am a Minister.

The Protestant: Are you a minister? why weare you not then
a Priest-cloake with sleeues, as you are injoyned in the
late *Booke of Cannons and constitutions Ecclesiasticall?* I took
you for one of the Burgesses, being you differ not from
them in habit.

The Puritane: What reason is there, that the fashion and
form of Ministers attire should bee different from other
mens?[12]

The battle soon moved from forms of dress to direct con-
frontation with civil authority. In general Separatists and
early Baptists were willing to accept civil authority in non-
faith matters. John Smyth, for example, noted in his work
A Short Confession of 1610, the necessity of acceding to the
magistrates in "worldly" matters.[13] Thomas Helwys echo-
ed these sentiments in *A Declaration of Faith of English People*
of 1611. The London Confession of 1644 supported the
right of civil authority in worldly affairs. Conflict arose
when the civil authorities tried to govern in religious matters.

Thomas Helwys wrote a work which directly challenged
the right of the king to speak in matters of faith. The work
was published in the early 1600's under the title *A Short
Declaration of the Mistery of Iniquity.* In the introduction ad-
dressed to the king, Helwys said:

The king is a mortall man, & not God; therefore hath no
power over ye immortall soules of his subietts, to make
lawes & ordinances for them, and to set spirituall Lords
over them. If the king have authority to make spirituall

Lords & lawes, then he is an immortal God, and not a mortall man.[14]

Helwys argued that, since the king had not power over souls, the people should be free to worship as they wished. The civil authorities should not wield the sword in the church.

Many others added their voices to that of Helwys. In 1610 John Robinson published *A Justification of Separation from the Church of England.* He argued that the king governed in civil matters but not in ecclesiastical realms. John Clarke published his famous book *Ill-Newes From New England* in 1652. He said that "no servant of Jesus Christ hath any authority from him to force upon others either the faith or order of the Gospel of Christ." One of the most outspoken critics of civil authority intruding in the church was Roger Williams. His book *The Bloudy Tenant of Persecution* emphatically denied that any authority was legitimate in the church other than persuasion. He noted, "God requireth not an uniformity of Religion to be inacted and inforced in any civill state; which inforced uniformity (sooner or later) is the greatest occasion of civill Warre."

Many early Separatists and Baptists appealed to conscience as a form of authority legitimate to faith. For example, the 1644 London Confession states, "So it is the magistrates duty to tender the liberty of men's consciences . . . and we believe it to be our express duty, especially in matters of religion, to be fully persuaded in our minds of the lawfulness of what we do."

The foremost source of authority accepted by early Baptists was the Bible. The Second London Confession of 1677 had two articles on biblical authority. The confession noted that Scripture conveys full divine authority and that any matter important to life and faith is dealt with in the Bible. This is a matter still very much in discussion today.[15] Since this book is not on this issue, I will not spend time and space here defending the Bible. That would be like a fire-cracker defending an A-bomb! I simply offer my opinion that the major disagreement about the Bible among Baptists today is not over its authority but over its nature and interpretation. Its authority is like Jesus' authority: It is self-authenticating.

Other early Baptists appealed to the association for authority. The first Baptist association in America dates back to 1707. This group offered guidelines for the congregations to bring disputes to the annual meeting for resolution of the problems.[16] The association offered itself as a mediator in the dispute. That tone has been generally followed since then.

Hearing the Word Today

This chapter began by asking, "Why do we do what we do?" This is a question of motivation and our perception of the authority that motivates us. Jesus spoke with authority that came from the essence of who He was. Christians today do not have the same sort of authority. Regardless of how much we love God and want to serve Him, we simply are not of the same ilk as Jesus. The best we can do is to live in close harmony with God as we are led by the Holy Spirit. The authority we follow is internal, not external. As someone noted, "The church as a spiritual democracy recognizes no authoritative principle but that which creates it as Christ's body, namely the Word, the Gospel, and the Spirit under Jesus Christ's lordship."[17] That is the authority which makes us follow day after day. That is the motivation which helped one rural preacher pray:

> Lord, give me a backbone as big as a saw log and ribs like the sleepers under the church floor. Put iron shoes on me and galvanized britches. Give me a rhinoceros hide for a

skin, and hang a wagonload of determination up in the gable end of my soul. Help me to sign a contract to fight the devil as long as I've got a fist, and then bite him as long as I've got a tooth, and then gum him until he dies.

Nothing from the outside could make him say that, and nothing external can force a person to believe. But faith, once initiated, is self-validating and authenticating. We don't have to footnote that, either.

Notes

1. See Tal D. Bonham, *Humor: God's Gift* (Nashville: Broadman Press, 1988).

2. G. B. Caird, *Saint Luke,* The Pelican New Testament Commentaries (Baltimore: Penguin Books, 1963), 219.

3. Werner Georg Kummel, *The Theology of the New Testament,* translated by John E. Steely (Nashville: Abingdon Press, 1973), 52.

4. Gunther Bornkamm, *Jesus of Nazareth,* trans. Irene and Fraser McLuskey with James M. Robinson (New York: Harper & Row, 1960), 57.

5. This is the conclusion of Edgar J. Goodspeed, *A Life of Jesus* (New York: Harper & Brothers, 1950), 172.

6. This is the conclusion of Larry W. Hurtado, *Mark,* a Good News Commentary (New York: Harper & Row, 1983), 177.

7. This is the conclusion of Frank Stagg, *Studies in Luke's Gospel* (Nashville: Convention Press, 1967), 119.

8. C. H. Dodd, *The Founder of Christianity* (New York: Macmillan Publishing Co., 1970), 148.

9. P. T. Forsyth, quoted by Morris Ashcraft, "The Issue of Biblical Authority," *Faith and Mission* v. 1, N 2 (Spring 1984): 25.

10. Russell H. Dilday, Jr., *The Doctrine of Biblical Authority* (Nashville: Convention Press, 1982), chap. 1. He credits Bernard Ramm with this list.

11. This story, and many other excellent teaching stories, is told in William J. Bausch, *Storytelling: Imagination and Faith* (Mystic, Conn.: Twenty-Third Publications, 1984), 62-63. Three other books with many

stories include these by William R. White, *Speaking in Stories* (Minneapolis: Augsburg, 1982), *Stories for Telling* (Minneapolis: Augsburg, 1986), and *Stories for the Journey* (Minneapolis: Augsburg, 1988).

12. Cited in Horton Davies, *The Worship of the English Puritans* (Glasgow: Dacre Press, 1948), 47-48.

13. This confession is printed in William J. Lumpkin, *Baptist Confessions of Faith* (Valley Forge: Judson Press, 1969, rev. ed.), 111.

14. Thomas Helwys, *A Short Declaration of the Mistery of Iniquity,* facsimile ed. (London: The Kingsgate Press, 1935 reissue), xxv.

15. See, for example, Ashcraft, 25-35; Roy L. Honeycutt, "Biblical Authority: a Treasured Heritage!" *Review and Expositor,* v. 82, no. 4 (Fall 1986): 605-622. Two books are also helpful in getting a feel for the discussion of the authority of Scripture: *Authority and Interpretation: a Baptist Perspective,* ed. Duane A. Garrett and Richard R. Melick, Jr. (Grand Rapids: Baker Book House, 1987), and *The Unfettered Word: Southern Baptists Confront the Authority-Inerrancy Question,* ed. Robinson B. James (Waco: Word Books, 1987).

16. See A. D. Gillette, ed., *Minutes of the Philadelphia Baptist Association from A.D. 1707, to A.D. 1807* (Philadelphia: American Baptist Publishing Society, 1851), 25.

17. *The New International Dictionary of the Christian Church,* s.v. "authority."

4

WEDNESDAY

Extravagant Love

Love does not stop nicely to calculate the less or more; love does not stop to work out how little it can respectably give. With a kind of divine extravagance love gives everything it has. —William Barclay

If you had only two days to live, how would you spend your time? It's a question worth thinking about because we never know how much time we do have. Some people would make amends for wrongs done to others. Some might rush to straighten out financial and inheritance matters. Still others might decide to live it up for a short while —trying everything they secretly had wanted to do but never before had the courage to try. Others might use their last forty-eight hours to do something noble for others who are less fortunate.

On Wednesday of what we call Holy Week, Jesus knew He had only two days to live. He knew what would happen to Him on Passover. He had alienated too many influential people. His action in the Temple with the whip among the tables and animal sellers had pretty well signed His death warrant.

Friday and its events would not catch Him off guard. Even so, with the knowledge of what would occur in two short days, Jesus chose to spend the last Wednesday of His life in seclusion in Bethany with close friends. Bethany was

about two miles from Jerusalem. Instead of making a foray
into the city, Jesus felt the need for a quiet time away from
the throngs which mobbed Him.

A Forbidden Setting

The Gospel of Mark tells us Jesus spent the time at the
home of Simon the Leper. He was probably a man whom
Jesus had cured, but who still carried the name "Leper."
Even so, Simon's home was somewhat a forbidden setting.
In that day, most people did not associate those who had
leprosy. They were afraid of catching the disease, and social rules prohibited contact between the clean and the
unclean.

But Jesus sat at the table of one whose whole life was
more than a skin disease. Jesus saw lives as more than
outward circumstances. To him, for example, Zacchaeus
was more than a shyster and traitor. He was a potential
member of the kingdom of God. A woman Jesus met beside
a well one afternoon was more than a person of questiona-
ble morals. She was a child who had lost her way but who
radiated with new life as Jesus gave her a drink of living
water.

Jesus saw more in His own disciples than others might
have seen. Simon Peter, for example, was not merely a
fisherman. He was literally a "little rock"—a solid man who
uttered a great confession. (Jesus is the big stone.) He was
not an "unclean" man because God chose to use him. Even
so, Simon would learn a painful lesson later when God
Himself would say to him, "Do not call anything impure
that God has made clean" (Acts 10:15).

And us? Are we not more than the total of our circumstances? Why do we fret and stew about life when Jesus
came to straighten the crooked, to mend the broken, and
to lift up the downtrodden? (Luke 3:4-5). He once said, "It
is not the healthy who need a doctor, but the sick" (Matt.

9:12). Our Great Physician sits at every table where He is invited to cleanse and heal.

An Ironic Recognition

Jesus sat in this socially forbidden setting, at table with Simon the Leper, better known to the Lord as Simon the Friend. There was no shame or wonder about proper social manners there. There was just the Master and friends. Other people came and went as word of Jesus' presence spread. His reputation as a healer and wonder-worker spread far and near. Though many people had already turned their backs on Him (John 6:66), the curious and the grateful looked for Him.

As Jesus and his friends sat cross-legged around the low table a strange thing happened. A woman seemed to come from nowhere and slip up behind Jesus. She had a small jar of perfume in her hands. She broke the jar and poured its entire contents over Jesus' head. Can't you just see it? Poor Simon nearly had a coronary! The disciples were shocked at this action because it seemed so forward, so inappropriate. Why would she have done such a thing?

The answer, in short, was that she knew who Jesus was. She might not have known all about what later generations called His divinity. The woman might not have been able to talk about the fact that Jesus was the Messiah. One thing she did know, however, and that was in Jesus she found someone special, Godlike, and unique. There is something ironic in this recognition. A woman, whose name we do not even know, found something in Jesus that called forth her complete devotion and extravagance. She had recognized in Him some quality that seemed to proclaim, "I am here on your behalf."

The New Testament as a whole treats this matter of recognition with an ironic touch. Jesus was recognized for who He was in a wide variety of ways. The so-called outcasts, like Simon the Leper, saw in Him a person who welcomed them with open arms. The elements of nature recognized His power over them and obeyed Him. He could calm a storm at sea, for example. (See Luke 8:22-25.) Even the demons knew and feared him. (See Mark 5:11-13.) Matthew, a tax collector, found what acceptance was; He accepted Jesus in return. A woman taken in adultery who was dragged before Him found a kind word when He stooped to write in the sand while her accusers thought about their actions. Perhaps He wrote, "Where is the *man?* Adultery requires two people." (John 8:1-11). Even a thief who hung on a cross beside Jesus knew Him.

That pattern repeats itself time and again in the Gospels. The little people, the nobodies, the strange, the unusual, the outcasts, the afflicted—these all found in Him something compelling and inviting. I am haunted by the idea that many people claim to find more openness and acceptance at the local pub than at the local church. Sometimes that is probably true!

After the fourth century, Christian artists began adding new figures to paintings of the Nativity. What they added were an ox and a donkey. This came from their interpretation of Isaiah 1:2-3:

> Hear, O heavens! Listen, O earth!
>   For the Lord has spoken:
> 'I reared children and brought them up,
>   but they have rebelled against me.
> The ox knows his master,
>   the donkey his owner's manager,
> but Israel does not know,
>   my people do not understand."

The Lord is known by even the ox and the ass, but ignored by many people!

The woman with a bottle of expensive perfume knew.

Something had happened in her life, and she would never be the same. The difference came about because of the itinerant Teacher from Galilee. This unknown lady's action underscores the irony of Jesus' reception in His world. The animals knew Him, and the demons knew Him; the elements of nature knew Him, and the down-and-outs knew Him. But His own people did not know Him. Let the church be very careful!

Today many still scoff at the whole idea of Jesus. They treat His name with contempt and use it as a curse. They make tasteless jokes about Him and use Him as the butt of gross stories. It makes no difference, though, because one cannot laugh God out of existence or joke one's way out of moral responsibility. Paul said that some day every knee will bow to Christ (Phil. 2:9-11).

One man whose life had been changed by a saving experience with Christ was laughed at by his fellow workers. He had been a heavy drinker who spent his paychecks on booze. "Hey, you really don't believe in miracles do you?" they would taunt. "Do you accept the story about Jesus turning water into wine?" He thought for a moment and said, "I can tell you this. He has turned beer into furniture!" The recognition of who Jesus is for us is the beginning of eternal life.

An Extravagant Gesture

How would you like a fifteen-thousand-dollar shampoo? Does that sound a little extravagant? It is, of course, but it is what the woman in this story gave to Jesus. She was carrying an alabaster jar of perfume extract which was to be used one drop at a time. But instead of rationing it a drop at a time, she impulsively snapped the neck off the bottle and poured the entire contents on Jesus' head.

It was an extravagant, even an insane, gesture. That essence was worth a year's wages to common working people.

Would you blow a full year's salary on one event? Any event? It is beyond comprehension. How would we pay the bills? Who would feed the kids? What about the taxes? The woman probably never asked such questions of herself. She simply acted impulsively but decidedly. There is a time for rational, methodical thinking. Someone has to look out after the bank account and keep the food on the table. But there is a time to act, to move out with feelings as well as with rational thinking. Few people get married by sitting down and saying, "Here are twelve reasons for our getting married, but here are twelve equally strong reasons for our not getting married. Let's flip a coin and see which it will be." In matters such as this, the heart—feelings—is as important as the mind—thinking.

This woman understood that something in the way Jesus looked at her, talked to her, and showed an interest in her was different from other men. I think He knew her before this incident at Simon's table. Somehow He had made some important difference in her life, and she wanted to repay the favor. Pouring a year's salary over His head may not have been smart, but it was intentional. Someone has said of love, it "never counts the cost. Calculation is never any part of love."[1] Paul said the same thing in what we call the "love chapter" of the Bible—1 Corinthians 13.

Listen to the way Paul spoke about this:

"Love is patient, love is kind. It does not envy, it does not boast, it is not proud. It is not rude, it is not self-seeking; it is not easily angered, it keeps no record of wrongs. Love does not delight in evil but rejoices with the truth. It always protects, always trusts, always hopes, always perseveres" (vv. 4-7). Love is God's gift which is broken and spilled out for our benefit. Love is our letting go of fear and opening ourselves up to the wonderful things God has for us. Love pours itself out extravagantly and does not hold back.

The Comanche Indians used to tell the story of their plea

to the Great Spirit during a great drought. The people called out, "O Great Spirit, our land is dying, and we are dying with it. Please tell us what we must do for You to end Your anger and send the rain." For three days the Comanches prayed this prayer and danced and waited. Then they waited some more, but no rain came. The drought was very hard on the little ones and the very old. Many people died.

One of the children who had not died was named She-Who-Sits-Alone. She watched her people pray and dance. The girl held on her lap a small doll which she treasured above all else. It was a warrior doll with a bone belt and beaded leggings. On its head were feathers from the blue-jay. She-Who-Sits-Alone spoke to her doll and said, "The wise men will go off to the hill soon. They will listen to the voice of the Great Spirit and will know what we must do to make the rains come."

She held her doll close to her heart as she talked. Her mother had made it for her, her father had brought her the feathers, and her grandparents had made the leggings. But that was long ago, and they were all dead from the drought and hunger. Her warrior doll was all she had from those happy days. As she talked to her doll, the wise men went to the hills to listen to the voice of the Great Spirit. After many days they came back and gathered the people of the village.

"The Great Spirit says that the people have become selfish," they reported. "For years they have taken from the land and have given nothing in return. So now everyone must make a sacrifice. The people must make a burnt offering of their most-valued possessions. The ashes of these offerings are to be scattered to the winds. When this is done, the rains will come again and will nurture life from the earth."

The people gave thanks to the Great Spirit for telling them what they had to do. All went to their teepees and searched for their most-valued possessions. One of the warriors said, "What shall I give? I'm sure the Great Spirit does not want my new bow." A woman mused, "I know the Great Spirit does not want my special blanket." This went on throughout the village. They had some excuse for keeping their most-valued possessions.

Everyone except She-Who-Sits-Alone. She held her warrior doll to her breast and said, "You are what the Great Spirit wants." She knew what she had to do. Later that night, when everyone else was asleep, She-Who-Sits-Alone crawled out from under her blanket, took a burning stick from the campfire and crept away to the hills. She climbed to the top of a hill, laid the burning stick on the ground, and spoke aloud. "O Great Spirit, here is my warrior doll. It is the only thing I still have from my mother and father. It is my most-valued possession. Please accept it."

The girl gathered some twigs and built a large fire. As she began to put the doll into the fire she hesitated. Tears rolled down her cheeks. But then she thought of her parents and all the others who died, so she dropped the doll into the flames. When the fire had died and the ashes cooled, she scooped them up and threw them to the winds to be scattered over the earth. By that time she was very tired, so she lay down on the ground and went to asleep. It was the first time she had slept without her doll, but she had a smile on her lips.

The sun woke her the next morning. She sat up, looked out over the hills, and was astonished. As far as she could see, the ground was covered with small beautiful blue flowers like tiny blue bonnets. They were as blue as the feathers in her doll's hair.

When the rest of the Comanches came out of their tents, they could hardly believe their eyes. They ran to the hill where She-Who-Sits-Alone had spent the night and stared in amazement at the flowers. There was no doubt in their eyes. The flowers were a sign from the Great Spirit that they were forgiven. They began to dance and sing and give thanks. And as they danced and sang, a gentle rain began to fall. The land itself seemed to wake from a long sleep, and the people were saved from starvation.

From that day on, She-Who-Sits-Alone was known as She-Who-Loved-Her-People. To this very day, in the land now called Texas, each year the Great Spirit remembers the love of the Comanche girl and covers the valleys with beautiful blue flowers.[2]

Love is generous to a fault. But extravagance was never so well spent as with Christ and an unnamed woman.

Hearing the Word Today

Why is there a critic in every crowd? Whatever you do, there is always someone standing around ready to say, "I told you so!" or "You should have done it my way," or "I knew it would never work." Even in this high and holy moment, when a woman acted out of deep love and devotion and poured out her best gift for Jesus, the critics spoke up. Mark 14:4-5 says, "Some of those present were saying indignantly to one another, 'Why this waste of perfume? It could have been sold for more than a year's wages and the money given to the poor.' And they rebuked her harshly."

But this "righteous indignation" didn't play. Jesus would have none of the sham. Look at his reply:

> "Leave her alone," said Jesus. "Why are you bothering her? She has done a beautiful thing to me. The poor you will always have with you, and you can help them any time you want. But you will not always have me. She did what she could. She poured perfume on my body beforehand to prepare for my burial. I tell you the truth, wherever the gospel is preached throughout the world, what she has done will also be told, in memory of her."

Worried about the poor? Great! You will have ample opportunity to feed and clothe them. But right now you had better attend to the business at hand. Poverty has no limit, but the presence of God in your midst as His Son is temporary. Jesus was saying, "Don't pour your cold water of skepticism on the embers of this woman's faith." Halford E. Luccock said about Jesus' comment, "There is evident here an excitement in Jesus, almost a lyric ecstasy, as though he felt: 'This is it. This is the self-forgetfulness, the self-denial, which is a mark of the kingdom of God.' "[3]

Some moments in life seem to come only once. This was one of them. Jesus wanted the critics and the skeptics to leave the dear lady alone, for she had done a beautiful thing in seizing the opportunity while she could. After all, had not the prophet Isaiah said, "Seek the Lord while he may be found" (55:6)? Some events and motives cannot be measured in dollars and cents. Some things in life are more important than the often-evoked bottom line. The love of the Savior is one such thing.

Jesus interpreted the anointing as preparation for burial. The broken pieces of the alabaster jar seemed to Him a symbol of what would soon be His own fate. He would be broken too. Like the woman's gesture, His brokenness would be an act of love. It would be a fragrance let loose in the world that would touch the nostrils of every person. Paul said on one occasion, "But thanks be to God, who always leads us in triumphal procession in Christ and through us spreads everywhere the fragrance of the knowledge of him. For we are to God the aroma of Christ among those who are being saved and those who are perishing. To the one we are the smell of death; to the other, the fragrance of life" (2 Cor. 2:14-16).

A bottle of expensive perfume impulsively poured out on the Savior was a sign of extravagant love both received and returned. I think the Lord still looks for that love in His people. I am certain He gives it.

A friend of mine was walking through a cemetery on Washington Avenue in New Orleans when he came across a tombstone of a man who died in 1866. The name on the stone was Telesphore Bourque. The inscription read, "Born December 29, 1830—Died April 11, 1866." A poem was also there:

> Why do we mourn for dying friends
> or shake at deaths alarms?
> This but the voice that Jesus sends
> To call them to his arms.
> Why should we tremble to convey
> Their bodies to the tomb—?
> There once the flesh of Jesus lay
> And left a long perfume.[4]

There is a fragrance that has been let loose in this world. It is a long perfume that has been broken and spilled out for all of us. Do you smell it?

Notes

1. William Barclay, *The Mind of Jesus* (New York: Harper and Row, 1960), 199.

2. This story is told in many forms. This particular story is from William J. Bausch, *Storytelling: Imagination and Faith* (Mystic, Conn. Twenty-Third Publications, 1985), 168-70.

3. Halford E. Luccock, *Interpreter's Bible* (New York: Abingdon Press, 1951), p 7:868.

4. My thanks to Perry R. Sanders, pastor of the First Baptist Church of Lafayette, Louisiana, for sharing this poem with me.

5

THURSDAY

Exemplifying Service

I try to give to the poor people for love what the rich could get for money. No. I wouldn't touch a leper for a thousand pounds; yet I willingly cure him for the love of God.   —Mother Teresa

My wife and I were driving through Arkansas on a Sunday when I was not preaching. I turned on the radio, and we heard five sermons that morning. Two impressed us. The first was from a well-established minister who has a national radio and television ministry. What he said that morning was suave, smooth, true to the Bible, and even somewhat interesting. But when it was over, it was over. It ended, and we could not remember much about it ten minutes later. The minister had spoken in generalities and used a lot of "Christian" language. The sermon was, thus, orthodox, but it had no staying power. It was "Generic Sermon 101."

The second sermon which impressed us was preached by a layman. He was filling in while the pastor was away that day. He was not quite as smooth and faultless in his delivery as the preacher we had heard earlier, but there was an important difference. He spoke from the Bible but made the message come alive as he poured himself into the sermon. He spoke of his granddaughter's recent death by drowning. He mentioned that early in his marriage his relationship with his father-in-law was strained. All of this came naturally from the passage of Scripture he was using as the text, and it covered the bones of the sermon's outline and gave it flesh and blood and laughter and tears. I was deeply moved by the layman's willingness to be specific about his situation and to struggle for answers as he spoke.

The difference between that first sermon and the second was the difference between the abstract concept "God loves us" and the concrete expression of that love: "God is with us while we stand at the graveside of our beloved grand-daughter." We need to hear both, of course. Even so, when someone wraps an abstract thought in a warm blanket of wiggling, cooing life, he has our attention. That is what God did on Christmas Day. On the final Thursday of His life, Jesus took the abstract notion of service and put life and movement into it.

Jesus had gathered His disciples together for a Passover meal.[1] He had sent them ahead to meet a certain man in Jerusalem who would be carrying a water jar. Since men in that era did not carry water—the women did—such a man would stand out in a crowd. Jesus had probably made arrangements with him earlier. When the disciples saw the man, they gave him the password in the form of a question: "The Teacher asks: 'Where is the guest room, where I may eat the Passover with my disciples?' " The man took them to his house to make the preparations. The Lord told His disciples, "I have eagerly desired to eat this Passover with you before I suffer. For I tell you, I will not eat it again until it finds fulfillment in the kingdom of God" (Luke 22:11-16).

Passover was the ceremony in which the Jews remembered how the death angel passed over them in Egypt. It was a very important religious holiday in Jesus' day. Being a committed Jew, He wanted to participate in it one last time.

Celebrating Salvation

The Passover feast was essentially a celebration of salvation from death.[2] It commemorated God's deliverance of the Jews from bondage. The English term comes from the Hebrew word *pesach* in Exodus 12:13: "I will pass over you. No destructive plague will touch you when I strike Egypt." The Jews knew of their escape from death. By the time of Jesus, the celebration had evolved into several specific steps which came in order.

The first was drinking from the cup of Kiddush. This act came first and separated this meal from all others. The head of the household took the cup and prayed over it. He then took a drink from it and passed it around for others to drink. Next came a special hand washing for the one leading in celebrating the feast. This was done three times. Following that, a piece of parsley or lettuce was dipped into salt water and eaten. The parsley stood for the hyssop with which the lintel had been smeared with blood. The salt water symbolized the tears of Egypt and the waters of the Red Sea through which the Jews escaped.

The breaking of bread came next. Two special blessings were used. Three circles of unleavened bread were on the table. The middle one was taken up, broken, and eaten. It reminded the family of the bread of affliction they ate in Egypt. The telling of the Exodus story came next. The head of the household recalled the experience of Israel in Egypt and of the escape. The story is essentially of the power and mercy of God. After the story came the singing of Psalms 113 and 114. This is part of the *Hallel* in Psalms 113—118, also known as "the Praise of God." Jewish youngsters had to memorize these psalms.

The second cup was then passed among the participants. It was called the cup of *Haggadah,* that is, the cup of explaining and proclaiming. Next came a general hand washing for everyone. Following that, grace was said over the unleavened bread. Small pieces were then passed. Bitter herbs were placed between two pieces of the bread and dipped in a mixture called *charosheth* and eaten. This mixture was a paste of crushed apples and nuts used to symbolize the mortar of brick making in Egypt. This bread was called the "sop."

The meal proper followed that. A whole lamb was roasted and eaten. Any leftovers were destroyed and not used in common meals later. Another hand washing followed the meal. The rest of the unleavened bread was then eaten. A prayer of thanksgiving was offered, and the third cup was drunk. Next, the second part of the *Hallel,* Psalms 115—118, was sung. The fourth cup was passed around and drunk, and the "Great *Hallel,*" Psalm 136, was sung. Two short prayers were offered, and the Passover feast ended.

Jesus and His disciples were familiar with this meal and probably participated in it every year. It helped define who they were as Jews and reminded them that their history was long and rugged. In Exodus 12:26 the children asked the parents, "What does this ceremony mean to you?" I can see the disciples asking Jesus something like that: "Lord, what does this meal signify to You? Why was it so important to You to eat it with us?" His reply in part was, "I have eagerly desired to eat this Passover with you before I suffer. For I tell you, I will not eat it again until it finds fulfillment in the kingdom of God" (Luke 22:15-16). We are not told if His disciples understood what He meant, but I think they did not. They were still pretty obtuse at this point of their pilgrimage.

Jesus gave the first cup in common and said, "Take this and divide it among you. For I tell you I will not drink again of the fruit of the vine until the kingdom of God comes" (Luke 22:17-18). That statement must have caught the disciples off guard. What could He mean? He explained by changing part of the Passover meal to meet His needs. Jesus took the unleavened bread, broke it after a prayer of thanks, and said, "This is my body given for you; do this in remembrance of me" (Luke 22:19). No longer was the Passover meal meant to be a backward look at their history. The disciples were to take this changed meal and use it as a signpost pointing toward the future. They were to remember, but then focus on their tasks for the future.

I have an "old-timer" pocketknife that belonged to my father. Every time I look at it, I cannot help but think of him. He was not a man of many personal possessions. He never had a record collection or personal library of favorite books. My dad was a simple man who kept only things like his clothes and his garden tools. The knife is special. It was uniquely his. I see it and remember that he never went anywhere without it. He used it to cut string when we went fishing together and to clean the catch. It was well used on his job in the oil fields of southern Louisiana. I see that old knife and remember his year-and-a-half struggle with lung cancer. It has so many associations for me that I can hardly begin to list them. It brings both smiles and tears. The Lord's Supper is like that. It may have become a staid and somber event in some modern churches, but it was not that originally. It used bread that reminded the Jews of slavery and tears and backbreaking work. It used wine, dangerous heady stuff that looked like blood. The disciples would never again have a Passover meal without thinking about that last meal with Jesus. They would remember the deep feelings, the strong emotions, the fear, and the hope. Our remembrance may never be that intense, but it can be a time of reflection that looks both backward and forward.

After passing out the bread, Jesus took the cup and blessed it and gave it a new interpretation: "This cup is the new covenant in my blood, which is poured out for you" (Luke 22:20). Through the prophet Jeremiah, God had

promised the coming of a new covenant—a new way of
relating between man and God. The prophecy reads:

> "The time is coming," declares the Lord,
>   "When I will make a new covenant
> with the house of Israel
>   and with the house of Judah.
> It will not be like the covenant
>   I made with their forefathers
> when I took them by the hand
>   to lead them out of Egypt,
> because they broke my covenant,
>   though I was a husband to them,"
>   declares the Lord.

The people had been unwilling, and possibly unable, to
keep the kind of covenant God had established with Moses.
Something had to be done, so God chose to rewrite the
terms and conditions of the covenant. Jeremiah 31:33-34
says that even its receptacle would be different:

> "This is the covenant I will make with
>   the house of Israel
>   after that time," declares the Lord.
> "I will put my law in their minds
>   and write it on their hearts.
> I will be their God,
>   and they will be my people.
> No longer will a man teach his
>   neighbor,
>   or a man his brother, saying, 'Know
>   the Lord,'
> because they will all know me,
>   from the least of them to the
>   greatest,"
>   declares the Lord.
> "For I will forgive their wickedness
>   and will remember their sins no more."

The basis of the covenant was no longer written law. The people of Israel had demonstrated for centuries that the law could not be kept. Paul wrote, "He has made us competent as ministers of a new covenant—not of the letter but of the Spirit; for the letter kills, but the Spirit gives life" (2 Cor. 3:6). Human beings who have limited freedom of choice and a conscience cannot be bound by mere do's and don't's. The bane of much modern Christianity is that it is based more on social mores than on grace. If one avoids certain things and attempts certain other things, one is looked on as a "good Christian." But where is the freedom to act as a responsible moral person before God? A religion consisting of do's and don't's tries to rewrite God's new covenant and make the original conditions binding again.

On that last Thursday of His life, Jesus gave to His followers a new act of celebration, remembrance, and anticipation. In Luke's account of this act, Jesus spoke of the new covenant but then immediately pointed out that one of the disciples would betray Him. He meant Judas, of course. In Matthew's account, the same thing happened, but something new is brought out. Jesus said, "I tell you the truth, one of you will betray me" (26:21). He also said, "This very night you will all fall away on account of me, for it is written:

> "I will strike the shepherd,
>   and the sheep of the flock will be scattered"
>   (26:31)

Judas's act was outright betrayal. The other disciples' actions were temporary lapses of faith but not betrayal. They "fell away" for a while, but they did not betray their Lord.

I take great comfort in that fact because I have had my times of lapses and falling away. Almost everyone who tries seriously to follow Christ has had these times. We may be thankful He does not hold these temporary reversals against us.

The Great Reversal

Many people seem to think that the entire universe revolves around them. They are so self-centered that they simply cannot see beyond their own skins. Years ago when *Look* magazine was in deep financial difficulties and about to go under, the management got all the employees together to explain the situation. After a detailed explanation of the crisis and the possible death of the magazine, the president of the company asked if there were any questions. One secretary raised her hand and asked, "Why doesn't the coffee-catering wagon stop on the thirteenth floor anymore?"

Something like that happened on that Thursday evening. Jesus had spoken with deep pathos about His coming suffering. He had graced His followers with a new symbol of remembering Him and of renewing their faith. The infamy of a traitor's work was exposed. Jesus spoke of His wishes for His followers. In all, the feelings in that upper room must have been deep and nearly overpowering. But look what happened next? "A dispute arose among them as to which of them was considered to be greatest" (Luke 22:24). How could Jesus have stood such immaturity and insult? I do not know! Here on the very eve of His death and at the moment when the relationship between God and humanity was about to be changed forever, the disciples were playing spiritual "king of the mountain." It was the ancient version of the secretary who wondered why the coffee wagon did not come her way anymore.

They were sidetracked and forgot the purpose of the evening. A man who used to live in Atlanta saw an advertisement for the "Church of God Grill." That piqued his curiosity, so he called the number listed. A friendly voice answered, "Hello! Church of God Grill." The caller asked why the restaurant had such an unusual name and was told this story: "Well, we had a little mission down here, and we started selling chicken dinners after church on Sunday to help pay the bills. Well, people liked the chicken, and we did such a good business, that eventually we cut back on the church services. After a while we just closed down the church altogether and kept on serving the chicken dinners. We kept the name we started with, and that's Church of God Grill."[3] The chicken remained, but the church died. A hunter told another version of this story. He had a deer hound which set off one morning chasing a magnificent buck. A few minutes into the chase, a fox crossed the path, and the hound veered off to chase the fox. A little later a rabbit crossed that path, and the hound was soon baying after the rabbit. Then a squirrel crossed the path and the dog pounded after him. Finally, a field mouse crossed the path, and the hound chased it into its burrow. The deer hound had begun chasing a great buck and ended up watching a mousehole.

The disciples disagreed about who was the greatest. How could Jesus answer a question like that? Would any answer really matter? To see Jesus' answer we may look at John's account of this night. John 13 says that when the meal was over Jesus took off His outer clothing and wrapped a towel around His waist. He poured water into a basin and began to wash the disciples' feet. Jesus usually taught by using word pictures and stories and symbolic acts. This washing was such an act. He seemed to be saying to the contestants in the power struggle, "Do you want to see genuine greatness in God's sight? Watch this."

Some commentators dismiss this aspect of the foot washing and claim that it was not about humility and service but about the cleansing action of Jesus' death.[4] I think that certainly was part of it, but the fact that Jesus would perform the task of the lowliest servant makes me think He was trying to show His disciples something about service. Luke said that Jesus asked the twelve, "Who is greater, the one who is at the table or the one who serves? Is it not the one who is at the table? But I am among you as one who serves" (22:27). In John's account, those words of Jesus were not recorded. Instead of preaching a sermon, He became one. His disciples got the message too. It was so pointed that impulsive Simon Peter could not contain his repulsion at what he saw happening. The Son of God, the Lord of all eternity, was on His knees and cleansed the dust off His followers' feet: Do you wish to be great? Then learn how to be humble and serve.

That fact repulses us too. I think William Temple was right when he wrote of this incident:

> We rather shrink from this revelation. We are ready, per-
> haps, to be humble before God; but we do not want Him to
> be humble in His dealings with us. We should like Him, who
> has the right, to glory in His goodness and greatness; then
> we, as we pass from His presence, may be entitled to pride
> ourselves on such achievements as distinguish us above
> other men.[5]

If our God is high and majestic, shouldn't His followers be also? But if God is ready to humble Himself, even to the point of being embarrassingly common, then what can His followers do?

What we can do is intentionally choose to be a servant. Robert Leslie said of Jesus' action, "In taking a towel and washing the disciples' feet, he was exercising his freedom to choose how to use his life."[6] I have the same sort of freedom *not* to be humble and serve God and others. If I cannot choose not to do it, then I cannot really choose *to* do it. I would simply be a puppet pulled by divine strings. That is not the case, however. Jesus said to the twelve after washing their feet, "I have set you an example that you should do as I have done for you. I tell you the truth, no servant is greater than his master, nor is a messenger greater than the one who sent him. Now that you know these things, you will be blessed if you do them" (John 13:15-17). He set the pattern. His service to them was to guide their service to others. It would become a pattern for their lives too. They would act like servants because they would be servants. The disciples would believe, but more than that—they would act like people who believe.

Leslie said of the faith that Jesus gave:

> The Christian faith has always been more than a system of belief. It is a way of life, a responsible and committed way of action. It is life lived under God, life derived from God, life reaching out toward God. The real secret of the personal ministry of Jesus can never be understood apart from his closeness to God. He found freedom for his life, as he first of all accepted personal responsibility in the search for meaning. And he found meaning as he exercised his freedom, under God, in service.[7]

This aspect of serving others is one of the toughest aspects of Christian life. I know of no greater heresy in Christianity today than the one which says, in effect, "I'm in this for what I can get out of it. God is going to give me anything I ask for. After all, Jesus said, 'Ask and you shall receive.'" This business of Get-rich-with-God is a terrible travesty being circulated by well-meaning but misguided people. Christ said, "Take up your cross," not "Fret over your C.D.'s and annuities." Besides, the matter of wealth is relative. A story from ancient Ireland reminds us of this fact.

Mochua was a hermit who lived alone. He had no worldly goods except for a rooster, a mouse, and a fly. The cock woke him in the morning in time for prayer. The mouse never let him sleep longer than a few hours. If he fell asleep while reading from his Psalter, the mouse nibbled at his ear until he awoke. The fly walked along each written line of the Psalter as Mochua read from it. When the hermit got tired of reading and singing the psalms, the fly rested on the line where Mochua left off. When the hermit was refreshed, the fly continued walking along the lines while Mochua read and sang.

So Mochua lived with his small flock of one rooster, one mouse, and one fly. After a time, his three precious ones died. Mochua was alone, so he wrote to his friend Columkille, sorrowing about his lost flock. Columkille wrote back to Mochua, "My brother, do not marvel that your flock should have died. For misfortune ever waits for those with too great a wealth."[8]

Hearing the Word Today

The church is not immune from the temptation to think of life in terms of what it can get rather than what it can give. A friend of mine was at an airport one day when he saw two elderly people at a counter. They each requested a wheelchair and some assistance, but choas broke out. Who would get the chairs? Who would push them to their departure gates? After much discussion, two young ladies went to the ramps where people board and came back with two wheelchairs. When they returned, however, they were informed that they could not use those chairs. The central office was sending two, and the count would be ruined if they used any others. The wrangling went on and on. The airline which had spent billions of dollars on equipment, personnel, and maintenance could not do even the most simple of tasks—assist two elderly people with wheelchairs. My friend who witnessed this comedy of errors compared it to what goes on in some churches. He wrote,

One cannot help but wonder how many people we leave

bewildered and confused because they have simple needs but the people in the church argue over how to meet the need, the theology of the need, the theology of meeting the need, the call to meet the need and how the need will be met. We have spent billions on buildings, personnel, programs and attracting people, then we can forget that above all else we are to meet the needs of people in a timely, Christian, redemptive manner.[9]

Ouch! That hurts because it is so true.

Thursday of Holy Week, the final week of Jesus' life, is often called Maundy Thursday. The word *maundy* comes from the Latin *mandatum*, the same word from which we get the word *mandate*. Christ's command—His mandate—in John 13:34 was that His disciples should love each other. How easy to say but difficult to do! Yet He had already shown how to do it when He donned the towel and knelt before each disciple.

We fear the idea of service because we think it may inconvenience us. Perhaps we fear that we will obligate ourselves to a long-term commitment and relationship which will tax our patience and strength. That might very well happen. Some of life's towels are long term. Dr. T. B. Maston taught Christian ethics at Southwestern Baptist Seminary in Fort Worth, Texas, for many years. Dr. Maston and his wife, Essie, were the parents of a son named Thomas McDonald. They called him Tom Mac. The boy was born with cerebral palsy. He never spoke a word, never fed himself, never controlled his bodily functions. He had to be helped with everything in his life. Tom Mac lived sixty-one years. He died of cancer. T. B. Maston and his wife made the decision not to put Tom Mac in an institution but to care for him at home. For sixty-one years they loved their son with action as well as feelings. I can hardly imagine that situation, but for them it was simply the right thing to do. They gave sixty-one years of love and service to their invalid manchild. Yes, some towels are for long-term use.

Others are emblazoned with the phrase, "For Short-term Use Only." These are the kind that *every* Christian should have in ample supply. When we are alert and living in each moment, we find all sorts of uses for these towels. Once as I was leaving a nursing home a resident standing in the lobby burst out laughing. She laughed and laughed so I stopped to see what was so funny. She was giggling at me! I walked over to her, and she said through her chuckles, "You look just like my old man!" (I was thirty-six at the time.) I started laughing. Then she said, "I sure wish I could hug you." I took a step forward and said, "Go ahead." That lady latched on to me with a hug I thought would send me to the chiropractor. She hugged and kissed me and laughed all the while. Finally she let go, waved good-bye, and chuckled as she shuffled down the hall. The sight of me triggered something in her memory, and I did not mind reminding her of her long-dead husband. Being hugged and sharing a laugh in a nursing home was a towel stroke that lasted no more than five minutes, but it was something I will never forget. It was a simple foot washing, but I came away with my feet clean too.

If life were simply comprised of "stuff," most Americans should be supremely happy. We have gadgets and gizmos piled high. A bumper sticker I saw recently said, "Life is a game, and the man with the most toys at the end wins." The most important phrase in that slogan is "at the end." Life does end, so playing games, accumulating junk, and chasing small slips of green paper does not make much sense. Bruno Bettelheim put it in these terms:

> Never before have so many had it so good; no longer do we tremble in fear of sickness or hunger, of hidden evils in the dark, of the spell of witches. The burden of killing toil has

been lifted from us, and machines, not the labor of our hands, will soon provide us with nearly all we need, and much that we don't really need. We have inherited freedoms man has striven after for centuries. Because of all this and much more we should be living in a dawn of great promise. But now that we are freer to enjoy life, we are deeply frustrated in our disappointment that the freedom and comfort, sought with such deep desire, do not give meaning and purpose to our lives.[10]

I think he is right. We are frustrated with life if all it offers is pampering and self-indulgence. Jesus could have had all that. In fact, during His temptations, He was offered just that—bread for His hunger, power, popularity—everything many people think would make them happy. A psychologist surveyed 287 college-age people. Almost every one of them said they wanted either "greatness" or "satisfaction" out of life.

Christ gave a different perspective on life. He chose a towel, and it became the only holy garment He ever wore. It became holy when he used it to wipe the dirt from His disciples' feet. It is the one vestment going begging in the modern church. I can't help but think that Jesus has one just our size.

Notes

1. There are technical problems involved with this. The Gospel of John differs from the Synoptic Gospels as to whether the meal was a Passover meal and on the time it was eaten. You may want to consult the technical commentaries to get a clear picture of the issues and possible solutions. I put the accounts together to form a picture of what actually happened on Thursday. The foot washing in John 13 seems to have taken place on Thursday. This is not a perfect chronology, but it is serviceable.

2. The bulk of this information comes from William Barclay, *The*

Gospel of Mark, The Daily Study Bible (Edinburgh: The Saint Andrew Press, 1956, 2nd ed.), 353-357.

3. Charles Paul Conn, *Making It Happen* (Old Tappan, N. J.: Fleming H. Revell, 1981), 95-96.

4. For this viewpoint see R. G. V. Tasker, *The Gospel According to St. John.* Tyndale New Testament Commentaries (Grand Rapids: Eerdmans, 1960), 155.

5. William Temple, *Readings in St. John's Gospel,* 1st and 2nd series (London: Macmillan Press, LTD, 1976 ed. [1940]), 209.

6. Robert C. Leslie, *Jesus as Counselor.* (New York: Abingdon Press, 1965), a Festival Book, 112.

7. Ibid., 123-124.

8. This story is from Robin Flower, *The Irish Tradition.* I read it in a letter from Robert Wilhelm's "Storyfest Ministry."

9. Lynn P. Clayton, "On Second Thought," *Baptist Message,* 22 January 1987, 4.

10. Bruno Bettelheim, *The Informed Heart: Autonomy in a Mass Age* (New York: Avon Books, 1960), preface.

6

FRIDAY

Enduring the Cross

*A lamb was chased by a wolf, and the lamb ran into a Temple.
The wolf said, "The priest would slay you if he catches you there."
The lamb replied, "It is better to be sacrificed to God than to be
devoured by you."* —Aesop

Menelik II was the emperor of Ethiopia from 1889 until
1913. News of a successful new means of dispatching crimi-
nals reached him. The news was about a device known as
an electric chair. The emperor eagerly ordered one for his
country. Unfortunately, no one bothered to warn him that
it would never work because Ethiopia at that time had no
electricity. Menelik was determined that his new purchase
should not go to waste. He converted the electric chair into
a throne.[1]

There was another occasion when an instrument of death
became a throne. On a Palestinian hillside about twenty
centuries ago, a cross became a throne for one named Jesus
of Nazareth. To this day that ancient instrument of torture
and death is converted into a powerful symbol of life, hope,
and resurrection. Millions of people around the world see
the cross as God's way of indicating His refusal to let death
and destruction have the final word.

On the last Friday of His life, Jesus was faced with a heavy
choice: to continue and fulfill His mission or to abort it and
save His life. Late on Thursday night, Jesus had been with

His disciples in Jerusalem for a meal in celebration of the Passover. He changed portions of that meal and reminded the twelve that they would never participate in it again without remembering Him. After the meal was completed, Jesus took the eleven—Judas left alone to complete his grisly task—and went to the Mount of Olives to pray. The hours to come would be the climax of all He had been about during His entire life.

Gethsemane

A part of the Mount of Olives was an area known as Gethsemane. Jesus took the eleven into this grove and stationed eight of the disciples by the outer edge. His instructions were simply, "Sit here while I pray," (Mark 14:32). Then he took the three who composed the inner circle among the disciples—Peter, James, and John—and went further into the garden. There Jesus began to feel the enormous pressure He was under. The ride into Jerusalem astride the ass, the cleansing of the Temple, the controversy with the authorities, the immaturity of His disciples as they argued over their positions in the kingdom—all of these events and struggles weighed heavily on His mind.

Mark said, "He began to be deeply distressed and troubled." These are words which suggest in the Greek deep feelings and inner turmoil. Jesus was a man pained by the events He saw around Him and by the fate He knew was in store for Him. The irony of the Gospels is that they portray Jesus as a man who came to give His life to save men, but also as a man who did not want to die. Let me explain. Jesus, as a real man, valued life and so did not want to waste His life and throw it away on nothing. He was, though, more than a man. He was ready to willingly surrender His life for a higher good. In the garden that late Thursday night and early Friday morning, Jesus wrestled with temptations much like those He faced at the beginning of His ministry. We generally refer to Jesus' temptations as being the ones which came as He began His public preaching ministry. I think that the experience in Gethsemane was as real a temptation as the ones several years earlier. Should He escape or stay and face the consequences? Could He do more good by living or by dying? Was God's will His sacrifice or His life? As He struggled with those questions, "his sweat was like drops of blood falling to the ground" (Luke 22:44). Something momentous and powerful was going on that night!

The inner conflict and the outcome of the struggle was paradoxical. On the one hand, Jesus had come in order to give His life. On the other hand, He was free not to give it but to escape from Jerusalem and continue to live. Only by being free *not* to die was He free *to* give His life willingly. He prayed in all seriousness, "Father, . . . everything is possible for you. Take this cup from me" (Mark 14:36). But then came the great "yet": "Yet not what I will, but what you will." That willingness to do God's will is what made the difference. Most people want to cling to life at all costs and will do almost anything to escape death. We do well to consider an ancient Persian story about a rich man who was walking in his garden with a servant. The servant cried out that he had just encountered Death who threatened him. The servant begged his master for the use of his fastest horse so the servant could flee to Teheran which he could reach that night. The master consented, and the servant galloped off at full speed. On returning to the house the master himself met Death and questioned him, "Why did you terrify and threaten my servant like that?" Death said, "I did not threaten him. I only showed surprise in finding him here when I had planned to meet him in Teheran tonight."

Whatever else the Gethsemane experience might have been, it was at least Jesus' absolute victory in following His

Father's will to its completion. The integrity which had given Him authority on Tuesday also carried Him through Friday. He prayed to maintain that integrity and urged His disciples to join the vigil. Three times the disciples fell asleep at their posts that night. They had just eaten a full Passover meal. Perhaps they were physically sluggish. The emotional stress of the week's events surely pulled on them too. Whatever the reason, those closest to Jesus could not stay awake long enough to support Him with their prayers.

Arrest and Trials

The action in the Gospels at this point is compressed like a steel spring in a box. There is abundant potential energy stored there. Actions were swift if not too certain. Decisions were made in a hurry. People gave their support to dark and dubious work. Political intrigue was at its height. Some reached Faustian bargains for the sake of power. Many were confused. A few were crushed. In the end, only one man stood out with His integrity intact.

The arrest of Jesus was accomplished easily enough. He was exactly where Judas had told the authorities to find Him. The traitor's kiss sealed the transaction and made the silver jingle in his pocket. Above all, the events of the arrest and the "trials" are full of ironies, illegalities, contradictions, and tragedies. Consider some of these.[2]

The first tragedy was that Jesus was the victim of a plot by the Pharisees to incriminate him.[3] Matthew 12 tells how Jesus healed a man on the sabbath. Verse 14 reads, "But the Pharisees went out and plotted how they might kill Jesus." Judas decided to lend support to this infamy by tipping off the Pharisees so they could arrest Jesus. We read that he began after Jesus' anointing at Bethany: "Then Judas Iscariot, one of the Twelve, went to the chief priests to betray Jesus to them. They were delighted to hear this and promised to give him money. So he watched for an opportunity to hand him over" (Mark 14:10-11). The plot also involved others who would serve as witnesses against Him. Their collusion broke down, however. When Jesus was before the Sanhedrin, "Many testified falsely against him, but their statements did not agree" (Mark 14:56).

A second tragedy on that Friday was that Jesus was the victim of evaded responsibilities. After His arrest, Jesus was hauled before six groups or persons for His "trials." The first was Annas. He was a former high priest and the father-in-law of the current one, Caiaphas. Annas worked behind the scenes and pulled strings quietly. The fact that Jesus was taken to him was very unusual, but Annas had arranged it. He probably had owned the stalls in the Temple which Jesus overthrew when He cleansed it. Annas had a chance to gloat over the bound Jesus. He could not actually do anything, however, so Annas sent Jesus to His next stop.

Jesus was then taken before Caiaphas the high priest. This was possibly a preliminary hearing used to examine Jesus. Those who plotted against Him still did not have all their charges ready. They probed and questioned, trying to get evidence they could use against Him. They finally came up with a charge of blasphemy.

Caiaphas sent Jesus on to the Sanhedrin. This group met early on Friday morning to consider what to do with Jesus. There was no sense of justice, for they had their minds made up already. As far as they were concerned, Jesus was a good as dead. After questioning Him, members of the Sanhedrin became enraged at Jesus' claim to be the Christ. They spat upon Him, beat Him, and verbally abused Him. This group sentenced Jesus to death, but it had no power to carry out the sentence. They sent Him to the Roman authority for that job.

Pilate was the fourth person to see Jesus. He was the Roman procurator, but he seemed to be well aware of the religious climate. Mark said Pilate knew it was for envy that the chief priests had handed Jesus over to him (15:10). He comes across in the Gospels as a man who clearly believed that Jesus was not a threat to him. His wife had a dream and told Pilate, "Don't have anything to do with that innocent man, for I have suffered a great deal today in a dream because of him" (Matt. 27:19). Even so, Pilate would not simply let Jesus go free. The procurator, who was supposed to be in charge, turned to those over whom he ruled and asked regarding Jesus and Barabbas, "Which one do you want me to release to you?" He evaded his responsibility to be a ruler and allowed the mob to choose. Pilate learned that Jesus was a Galilean and, therefore, under Herod's jurisdiction. He sent the prisoner to Herod. It was a convenient way to pass a political/religious hot potato without getting burned—or so he thought.

The interview before Herod was the fifth for Jesus. Herod Antipas was the son of Herod the Great and tetrarch of Galilee and Perea. He was delighted to have a chance to meet Jesus, for he had heard often of Him. The reason for his delight was simple: "He hoped to see him perform some miracle" (Luke 23:8). This was good fun and sport, like a circus. "Now, Jesus of Nazareth, let's see You turn some water into wine. Or how about curing one of my lame servants? That shouldn't be too hard for You, should it?" Herod ridiculed and mocked Jesus and, when the laughter died away, sent Him back to Pilate.

Jesus went back before Pilate for His sixth interview or trial. Pilate, to his credit, gathered the people who made the accusations against Jesus and said, "I have examined him in your presence and have found no basis for your charges against him. Neither has Herod, for he sent him back to us; as you can see, he has done nothing to deserve death. Therefore, I will punish him and then release him." (Luke 23:14-16).

In all six of the so-called trials, one fact stands out. While everyone wanted to be in on the accusations, no one seemed very willing to take full responsibility for executing Jesus. The Sanhedrin hated Him but could not put Him to death. Pilate could have had Him killed easily, but he wanted no part of it. Instead, he shuffled Jesus off to Herod for the dirty work. Herod enjoyed the sport, but he would not condemn Jesus either, so he marked Him "return to sender" and sent Him back. Even the second time, Pilate wanted no trouble with Jesus. Evaded responsibilities were part of that last Friday.

Jesus' treatment at the hands of the Sanhedrin was illegal.[4] It was illegal because the court which was to decide His case was also an accomplice in His betrayal. They set a trap for Him and tried to trick Him into incriminating Himself. In no sense was that court impartial and fair. Next, the trial did not begin with a statement of the specific charge against Jesus as their law stipulated. In fact, they had difficulty in coming up with a specific charge because the witnesses were so unreliable. That fact should have made the court acquit Jesus, but that did not happen.

Further, the judge trying the case was a leader for the prosecution. Caiaphas filled both roles, so any possibility of Jesus getting a fair hearing was zero. He had already said publically, "It is better for you that one man die for the people than that the whole nation perish" (John 11:50). Another reason for the illegal nature of the trial was that no witnesses for the defense were called. No one spoke up in Jesus' behalf or tried to explain His statements and actions. The only voices heard were of the prosecution. Finally, the most glaring aspect of the trial was its speed. Jewish law stipulated that twenty-four hours had to pass between the time someone was found guilty of a capital case and the time the actual sentence was given. A full day had to elapse. Also, no case was to be heard on the day before the sabbath or a great festival. The accusers of Jesus that Friday broke their own laws and disregarded normal procedures for going about their business. The trial itself, then, was illegal and not in accordance with Jewish custom. It was just one more sham that was done on the day of Jesus' crucifixion.

One irony of Friday was the making of strange bedfellows. On that day, groups and individuals who usually disliked each other came together. Various factions within the Sanhedrin sometimes argued among themselves, but they solidified in their opposition to Jesus. Of two prominent politicians, we read, "That day Herod and Pilate became friends—before this they had been enemies" (Luke 23:12). D. R. Davies has noted that this friendship was inevitable because of the one whom they united to fight. Such a battle takes great strength. "The relative distinctions *within* society merge into the absolute opposition of the whole society. . . . Men always remain divided against one another. It is only against God that they unite."[5]

Another travesty of Friday was the betrayal of sacred trusts. In John's version of the trials, Pilate tried to set Jesus free. He realized that Christ was innocent of political subversion. When Pilate suggested to the Jews that he would release Jesus, they responded with a most telling answer: "If you let this man go, you are no friend of Caesar. Anyone who claims to be a king opposes Caesar" (19:12). There it was—the ace up their sleeve. They threatened Pilate with political pressure. They would go over his head and take the matter directly to Caesar. The mighty Caesar would not be pleased if he learned that his person in charge could not handle things. The horrible thing about the Jews' threat is that they were supposed to have only one king—the God of Israel. Their appeal to Caesar was a betrayal of a sacred trust. It showed that no longer where they most interested in what the Lord wanted. What they really desired was peace and stability at any cost. In desperation they cried out, "We have no king but Caesar" (19:15). Their appeal to Caesar was an act of idolatry as much as if they had called on Baal.

A further disaster on that Friday was the seeming triumph of mob mentality. Pilate wanted to release Jesus, but the crowds, stirred up by the chief priests, would not hear of it. Luke said, "With one voice they cried out, 'Away with this man! Release Barabbas to us!" (23:18). Matthew said that when Pilate supported Jesus' innocence and refused to have His blood on his hands, "All the people answered, 'Let his blood be on us and on our children!'" (27:25). The anonymity of the crowd and the frenzied whipping up of hate and violence seemed to have had the last word.

One other Friday anomaly should be noted. That is the atmospheric and geologic disturbances. Matthew reported an earthquake (27:50-53). Luke reported a midday darkness which spread over the land like a giant blanket (23:44-46).

The last day of Jesus' life was thus full of travesties of justice, the rule of a mob mentality, and the betrayal of a people's deepest beliefs. Unusual alliances were formed, and former enemies came together. Even nature itself seemed disturbed.

The Cross and Atonement

"They led him away to crucify him," (Matt. 27:31). It seems so calm, so cruel and cold-blooded. And, of course, it was. Many people in that day were crucified by the Romans. It was gruesome punishment and public humiliation. It was supposed to deter people who thought about challenging Rome. While crucifixion probably did dissuade many, others lived as they wanted to and accepted the threat of the cross.

The cross was the Roman instrument of public execution. Something remarkable happened to it, though, when a Galilean carpenter was spiked to it. The instrument of death and humiliation became God's method of bringing people back to Himself. As Paul said many years later, "God chose the foolish things of the world to shame the wise; God chose the weak things of the world to shame the strong. He chose the lowly things of this world and the despised things—and the things that are not—to nullify the things that are" (1 Cor. 1:27-28). Who would have thought about a cross becoming an instrument of salvation and good? Some of the prophets had spoken about the Suffering Servant and the Messiah who would be rejected, but not even the prophets could have imagined the disgrace and contempt which Jesus endured. God chose to use the most despised symbol of death and subjection as His supreme instrument of life and resurrection.

We humans have a fatal flaw. We are lost and cannot save ourselves. We simply cannot pay the price. Even if we could, who would be willing? We are like a slave in the antebellum South named Tom. His owner allowed Tom to take jobs off the plantation at night, on holidays, and on weekends. He worked hard for his owner and then would walk fifteen miles into town, work there, and return home. After two hours of sleep, Tom would repeat the action. This went on for years, and he saved every penny. He refused to marry but spent every waking hour working. After he saved a thousand dollars, Tom went to his owner and asked how much he was worth. The man said that most slaves brought from between eight to twelve hundred dollars. However, since Tom was getting old and did not have any children, if he wanted to buy himself, the owner would let him go for six hundred dollars. Tom thanked his owner and went back to his cabin and dug up his money. He fondled the cash and remembered how long it took to get it. He put it back into its hiding place, went back to his owner, and said, "Boss, freedom is a little too high right now. I'm going to wait till the price comes down."[6]

The symbol of what God did for us when we could do nothing for ourselves is a cross. It took everyone by surprise when the church was no more than a gleam in God's eye. The cross has become the mode through which God gives Himself and, in a sense, defines Himself. I think Alister McGrath was right on target when he said, "All human conceptions of what 'God' must be like are shown up as inadequate and ridiculous, and we are thus humiliated through the failure of our reason and wisdom, and compelled to consider God as he has revealed himself in the crucified and dying Christ."[7] McGrath called the cross "the sole *authorised* symbol of the Christian faith." Exactly! What we know about God through Christ is filtered through the prism of the cross. It is mysterious, difficult to comprehend, and even embarrassing.

The cross changes the perspective from which we look at God. Perhaps I can explain it this way. I spent one July as visiting professor at Midwestern Baptist Seminary in Kansas City, Missouri. While in that city my family went to a Kansas City Royals baseball game one night. We were in the cheap seats that seemed about half a mile from the diamond. They were above and behind the catcher to his right. The pitcher would wind up and throw, the batter would swing, and the ball would streak away from the bat. From my perspective I would think, "That one is a high fly to center." It would actually be a line drive to the third baseman. Another hit would seem as if it would fall right on top of the shortstop, but it would actually go to right field. The perspective from which I was viewing it distorted my perception of the ball game.

Something like that happens in our understanding of God. Few people considered thinking about God from the perspective of suffering, degradation, and death. Yet, on the final Friday of His life, Jesus gave us a new angle of vision—a new way of thinking about God. He did choose the foolish and lowly as Paul had said. He showed us a side to Himself that no one had noticed before. As McGrath says, "The cross reveals the fundamental uncontrollability of God, who breaks the mould of our thinking."[8]

Even so, Christians have always tried to understand, at least a little, what God did on the cross to change people. This change is called the atonement. The atonement is the effect which the life, teaching, death, and resurrection of Jesus has on the life of those who will appropriate the power of those events into their own lives. This results in the forgiveness of sins at a personal level, a sense of power and victory over hostile forces, a sense of having been redeemed at an enormous cost, and the possession of an example to follow. Jesus, as the Christ of God, did for men and women what they could not do for themselves, namely, to become reconciled to God. This, in broad strokes, is the meaning of the atonement.[9]

But almost as soon as someone makes this affirmation one must begin to answer several questions about it: "How did this happen? Why was it necessary? What part did man play in this?" Robert Culpepper said, "The purpose of the atonement according to the New Testament, stated in the broadest terms, is to deal effectively with our sins in such a way as to deliver us from the penalty, power, and presence of sin, to reconcile us to God, and to bring moral and spiritual renewal by imparting a new principle of life and righteousness."[10]

Atonement is a word which refers to the reconciliation between humanity and God. The idea for such reconciliation is found throughout the Bible, both Old and New Testaments. In the Old Testament the foundations of the doctrine of the atonement are found in the concepts of election of Israel and the covenant.[11] The choice of God to elect the people Israel and to enter a covenant relationship with them reveals that God is interested in human well-being. Several other concepts frequently associated with atonement have their roots in the Old Testament. These include the idea of sacrifice, the concept of the Messiah, and the servant-of-God motif.

The concept of atonement is in the New Testament. That Christians would be concerned with the atonement is understandable but rather peculiar considering the scarcity of the word *atonement* in the New Testament. This word occurs only once in the *King James Version,* in Romans 5:11. This is a translation of the Greek word *katalaga.* In newer translations this word is usually not translated as "atonement" but as something else. The following list show some of these meanings:

"Reconciliation:" *New American Standard Bible,* Weymouth, Goodspeed, Williams, *New English Bible,* Phillips, *New International Version.*

"Friendship:" Beck translation

"God's friends:" *Good News Bible*

As is noted above, the word *reconciliation* is the most numerous choice among modern translations of the Bible. This is understandable since the word *katalaga* suggests adjustment or change in status, and thus reconciliation.

In his classic book *The Atonement in the New Testament.* Vincent Taylor suggested that fourteen images or ideas for the atonement are found in the New Testament.[12] These include the following:

1. The death of Christ was related to God's purposes.
2. The death of Christ was messianic in character.
3. The death of Christ was vicarious.
4. The death of Christ was representative; it includes us; in His death we die.
5. The death of Christ was related to our sin.
6. The death of Christ was sacrificial.

7. The death of Christ was interpreted in terms of the Suffering Servant.
8. The death of Christ is always related to the resurrection.
9. The atonement of Christ is appropriated by faith.
10. The death of Christ is illustrated in the Lord's Supper.
11. The idea of suffering with Christ is involved in His suffering.
12. His death is related to the love of God.
13. His death is related to moral and spiritual ends.
14. There is a universal aspect in Christ's death.

Other images or word pictures exist in the New Testament. These include the ideas that Christ's death is: perfect sacrifice (Heb. 9:26; 10:5-10); payment of sin's due penalty (Rom. 3:25-26; Gal. 3:13); redemption (Eph. 1:7); a price paid (1 Cor. 6:20); a new covenant (1 Cor. 15:55-57); propitiation (Rom. 3:25); reconciliation (Eph. 2:16); suffering as an example (1 Pet. 2:21).

In all of this discussion, we must be very careful to remember that the idea of atonement is itself a model or a word picture of what transpires between God and man. The Bible, and especially the New Testament, gives an overall view that fellowship between God and men was ruptured and that Jesus, through His life, death, and resurrection, restored that relationship. The relationship between God and humanity is best described as "at-one-ment." Jesus' life and death are, therefore, inseparably linked. To speak of Jesus' death is not simply to speak about an event when life left His body, but rather to speak of what He did in life and in death to repair the breach between God and human beings. To say this is not to suggest in the slightest that God was not interested in or capable of repairing this breech. Jesus did not work outside of

God's intentions but rather within them, for "God was reconciling the world to himself in Christ" (2 Cor. 5:19).

Hearing the Word Today

Studying various views of the atonement is helpful in grappling with what happened, but we must remember that salvation does not come by man's theorizing. To paraphrase a biblical saying, "Man does not live by speculation alone but by the redemptive act done by Jesus." On that Friday long ago, something happened to change forever the standing of persons with God. The theories about what happened are interesting and even vital, but when all is said and done, no theory can *fully* explain why the death of one person two millennia ago has the power to change my life today.

God decided to give Himself to humanity in a new way in the incarnation. He fully accepted the risk that people would react to His Son in exactly the same way people react to everything—some accept, some reject, some ignore. Even so, in love God gave Himself to bring us back to Himself. The results at first seemed like failure because the crucifixion appeared so permanent. Jesus died and was genuinely dead. That He would offer Himself that way is amazing and incomprehensible. George Herbert's old poem expresses it well:

> Love is that liqueur sweet
> and most divine.
> Which my God feels as blood
> but I as wine.

What is blood to God is life and joy to me!

Jesus accepted suffering as the way to bring people to God. Henry Nelson Wieman pointed out many years ago that pain and suffering are not the same thing. Suffering is a meaningful, communicable event. According to Wieman, emotional maturity is the willingness to incur suffering in order that creative good might emerge. Emotionally mature people do not necessarily seek suffering but recognize that it goes hand in hand with all genuine transformation.

Had Jesus merely wanted to save His life, He could have. But He had some goal in mind larger that His own life. He accepted the suffering on the cross in order for the transformation of sinful people to take place. When all is said and done, I really cannot explain that fact. I can only proclaim it.

Notes

1. From *The Little, Brown Book of Anecdotes*, Clifton Fadiman, general ed. (Boston: Little, Brown and Co., 1985), 396. On another matter, Menelik had an unusual belief. When he was sick, he would eat pages out of the Bible, and he thought it would cure him. Most of the time his odd habit did him no harm. In December of 1913, however, he was recovering from a stroke. He ordered that the entire Book of Kings be torn out of his Bible and fed to him page by page. He died before he finished the book.

2. Each of the Gospels gives a unique interpretation of the arrest and trials of Jesus, and His death and its meaning. I am working with all four Gospels here, but if you want to see their individual perspectives and emphases, consult these books: Raymond E. Brown, *A Crucified Christ in Holy Week: Essays on the Four Gospel Passion Narratives* (Collegeville, Minn.: The Liturgical Press, 1986); Reginald H. Fuller, *The Formations of the Resurrection Narratives* (New York: The Macmillan Co., 1971); and Frank J. Matera, *Passion Narratives and Gospel Theologies*, Theological Inquiries (New York: Paulist Press, 1986).

3. A clear explanation of these "trials" is given by William Barclay, *The Mind of Jesus* (New York: Harper and Row, 1960), chap. 25, and his *The Life of Jesus for Everyman*, a Harper Jubilee Book, (New York: Harper and Row, 1965), 56-61.

4. James S. Stewart, *The Life and Teaching of Jesus Christ* (New York: Abingdon Press, n.d.), 159-160.

5. D. R. Davies in *What the Cross Means To Me: a Theological Symposium* (London: James Clarke & Co., LTD, 1943), 42.

6. This story is told by Maya Angelou, *The Heart of a Woman* (New York: Bantam Books, 1981), 41-42.

7. Alister E. McGrath, *The Mystery of the Cross* (Grand Rapids: Zondervan Publishing House, Academie Books, 1988), 103-104.

8. Ibid., 104.

9. For more, see my article, "Toward an Understanding of the Atonement: an Historical and Interpretative Essay" in *Theodolite: a Journal of Christian Thought and Practice* V. 8, 1 (1987): 17-27.

10. Robert Culpepper, *Interpreting the Atonement* (Wake Forest: Stevens Book Shop, 1979 [1966]), 65.

11. Ibid, 19 *ff.*

12. Vincent Taylor, *The Atonement in the New Testament* (London: Epworth Press, 1940), 50-51. See also Morris Ashcraft, *Christian Faith and Beliefs* (Nashville: Broadman Press, 1984), Chap. 10.

7

SATURDAY

Experiencing Silence

We know there is some connection between prayer and silence, but if we think about silence in our life it seems that it isn't always peaceful; silence can also be frightening. —Henri J. M. Nouwen

"Joseph took the body, wrapped it in a clean linen cloth, and placed it in his own new tomb that he had cut out of the rock. He rolled a big stone in front of the entrance to the tomb and went away" (Matt. 27:59-60). This account of the burial of Jesus seems cold and curt. They laid Him in the tomb, and that was that. Everybody could get on with their lives. Pilate could go back to his political games. Herod could find amusement at someone else's expense. The Pharisees could rest content with the knowledge that they need not worry about that boat-rocking radical from Galilee. Or could they?

Something had happened the day before. Exactly what that something was could not have been known on Saturday. The people knew some of the obvious events. The earth shook, and the sky darkened. The curtain in the Temple which separated the "acceptable" people—Jews—from the "nonacceptable" people—the Gentiles—was ripped in two. The hopes of the families of three men were nailed to crosses. Followers ran away. One betrayed. Some laughed. Some cried. Many ignored. But *something* had happened, something that was not so obvious or which could be appreciated at the time. Consider some of the events of Saturday from the perspective of both people and God.

Saturday: From the Human Perspective

Seen from a human viewpoint, Saturday was both a tragedy and a triumph. The biblical record shows both of these aspects. Matthew's Gospel gives a glimpse at what went on late Friday night and on Saturday. Few people slept well on the night of the day Jesus died. His family and followers had witnessed His cruel execution. Surely they were restless that evening. The day had been full of chaos, heartbreak, terror, and dread of the unknown. Matthew 27:61 seems to indicate that Mary Magdalene stayed at the grave site all Friday night.

But Jesus' followers were not the only restless group that night. The Pharisees was another group whose memories of the day's events troubled their sleep. Why were they so restless? I think it was because they remembered Jesus' words about rising again. These Jewish leaders would not have understood the full import of Jesus' comment, but they had heard Him often enough to know that His words were never empty. They did not like much of what He said, but they at least took Him seriously.

In Matthew 27:63, Jesus is called a "deceiver." The accusation was that He was nothing like He claimed to be. The argument was futile, however. The matter of Christ's identity and His resurrection is not a debating point or a conclusion of finely plotted reasoning. Proofs of His identity are never given in the Bible. Anything that could be considered a proof about Jesus' divinity can be argued against. Only indications, signs, and pointers to truth are provided. After all, Christianity is a matter of faith. The New Testament gives indications about the resurrection faith, of course. Acts 1:3 speaks of Jesus' appearance to the disciples after

His resurrection. It reads: "After his suffering, he showed himself to these men and gave many convincing proofs that he was alive. He appeared to them over a period of forty days and spoke about the kingdom of God." The proofs were to those who already believed. To someone who refuses to believe, nothing is an irrefutable proof.

First Corinthians 15:3-8 also gives the core teaching of resurrection faith. In summary fashion, Paul spoke of the events of the death, burial, and resurrection of Jesus. This is not undeniable proof because many did deny, and still do. To people of faith, it is a good indication of what happened and why it happened. God does not bang people over the head and shout, "Believe!" Some people do have very dramatic divine encounters, but for most, coming to faith in Christ is a matter of gentle persuasion because persuasion is better than force.

Even nonreligious people know this. Aesop told the story of the wind and the sun getting into an argument over who was stronger. Below them they saw a man wearing a heavy coat. "Let us see who can strip the man of his coat the fastest," said the wind. The sun agreed and allowed the wind to go first. The wind came upon the man with a furious blast, causing his coat to flap around him. But the harder the wind blew, the tighter the man held onto the coat. Then the time came for the sun to try. The sun shone brightly upon the man who unbuttoned the coat. The sun just kept shinning warmly and fully, and in no time at all the man took off the coat and carried it over his arm.

We have the advantage of retrospect, but neither the disciples nor the politicians really knew what would happen next. Saturday from their viewpoint seemed like the end. For the disciples, it was the end of a magnificent dream. They had wanted so much, had hoped so deeply, had loved so completely. For the politicians, Saturday was the end of a nightmare. Even though they knew Jesus had died, still

they wondered about His words. The Pharisees quoted
Jesus' own words to Pilate. They remembered that he had
said, "After three days I will rise again." This was quite an
ironic scene. Just the day before, the Pharisees called for
blood, and Pilate satisfied their thirst. He handed Jesus
over to their demands for crucifixion. The events of that
Friday were still fresh in their minds on Saturday morning,
and they wanted to clear up a major problem with Pilate.

Saturday is the Jewish sabbath. For Jews to meet with a
political leader on the sabbath was *very* unusual. Why did
they do it? I think it was because they were troubled by what
they had heard Jesus say. The chief priests and others quoted Jesus' own words to Him during His trial. Matthew
26:61 reads, "This fellow said, 'I am able to destroy the
temple of God and rebuild it in three days.' " These words
troubled the Jewish leaders. They could not have fully understood what Jesus had meant by rebuilding the temple or
rising again, but their uneasiness was surely enough to have
kept many of them awake.

They did not accept the message which Christ had come
to proclaim, but they could not simply ignore it. There had
been suggested to their minds the possibility, just the *slightest* possibility, that Jesus might have been who He said He
was. That possibility worked on the consciences of some of
the religious leaders. They would not believe, but neither
could they ignore.

A similar situation exists for many people today. Among
my own friends I have some who are limping between two
great claims. On the one hand, they have heard the claims
of the Christian gospel and its promise of forgiveness and
eternal life. On the other hand, they are modern people
heavily influenced by secular values and culture. They do
not quite believe, but neither can they not write off the
gospel. Such a dilemma is tough. The denial of the resurrection of Christ stemmed from opposition to the message

He preached. We need to take full account of the fact that this sort of denial dates back to the first Easter. Unbelief is not a new phenomenon, but it is as old as resurrection hope and proclamation. The leaders could not bring themselves to believe. (Religious belief, in part, is a conscious decision). But they could not convince themselves that there was no truth in what Jesus had claimed. Living in this betwixt-and-between realm is uncomfortable at best, and intolerable at worst.

Intolerance, bigotry, power, and position had dealt the blows that ended Jesus' life. Every ringing of the mallet as it drove the spikes into Jesus' wrists was a sound accompanied by the silent grins of self-satisfied men. They had power and prestige. They had positions to consider, property to protect, and tradition to honor. What was it to them if one man, even if He were innocent, had to die?

The Gospel of John lets us eavesdrop on a meeting of the Jewish council as they discussed the "problem" of Jesus. Listen to their conversation:

> Therefore the chief priests and the Pharisees convened a council, and were saying, "What are we doing? For this man is performing many signs. If we let Him go on like this, all men will believe in Him, and the Romans will come and take away both our place and our nation." But a certain one of them, Caiaphas, who was high priest that year, said to them, "You know nothing at all, nor do you take into account that it is expedient for you that one man should die for the people, and that the whole nation should not perish" (John 11:47-50, NASB).

Here, in the most blatant terms, is the word of power and position which overlooks truth and prefers stability. "Better him than us!" The idea of sacrificing one for many is very old. What we Americans call the Great Wall of China, the Chinese call the Ten Thousand Li Long Wall. Shih

Huang-ti was the emperor who began the wall in the third century. The work was enormous and painfully slow. Sections of the wall kept crumbling. One of the emperor's counselors told him that they should entomb a workman ever mile so that his spirit might guard the wall against the wilderness. The emperor agreed and was ready to sacrifice ten thousand workmen. One scholar had a conscience, however. He told the emperor that one man named Wan would be enough, because Wan means "ten thousand." So they sacrificed Wan and buried him in the wall, thinking that the sacrifice of one was better than many. This sounds a bit familiar, doesn't it?

In some ways, human society has not moved too far from pharisaic attitudes. People are still interested in protecting themselves, and rightly so. But at what point can we lower the barriers and listen to the claims of others as they try to teach us something? I have an acquaintance who simply will not listen to others. This is one reason he is not much of a friend. Whenever I am around him, he dominates the conversation. If I tell of a trouble, he will tell of a greater problem. If I mention a fun experience, he will try to top it.

The trouble with the religious council in Jesus' day was more serious than the problem my acquaintance has, but it was fashioned on much the same sort of self-interest. The issue with the council went beyond mere protection and caution. It crossed over the line to a selfish and perverted reasoning, a reasoning that seemed to say, "We'll hold what we've got at all cost. Our interest is us and ours."

One of the best-loved hymns in many churches is entitled "O Master, Let Me Walk with Thee." It was written by Washington Gladden as a poem entitled "The Great Companion" and was later set to music. It has a second stanza which is not included in the hymn version.

O Master, let me walk with Thee
Before the taunting Pharisee;
Help me to bear the sting of spite,
The hate of men who hide Thy light,
The sore distrust of souls sincere
Who cannot read Thy judgments clear,
The dullness of the multitude
Who dimly guess that Thou are good.

While this may not be great poetry, it does describe an attitude which manifested itself in the chief priests and Pharisees.

On that Saturday in question, the action centered around the request by the Pharisees and priests to have Pilate guard the grave of Jesus. They wanted to discredit the claims of Jesus and His followers. To do this they claimed that Jesus' followers were unscrupulous people who would stop at nothing to promote His claims. The delegation visiting Pilate convinced Him that the followers of the executed man would steal His body and then claim that He arose from the dead. Then the "last deception will be worse than the first."

What was the first? To their thinking, Jesus' first deception was His claim to divine authority. Again and again they had asked him, "By what authority do you do these things?" (See Matt. 21:23; Luke 20:1-8; see also chap. 2 of this book.) This claim, according to the Pharisees, was nothing less than blasphemy. It was deception in their thinking and enough of an offence to have them plot Jesus' death.

They could not bear the thought of a second, more offensive, deception—having Jesus' body stolen from the grave and the claim made that He was alive. That would be too much, so they took measures to ensure it would not happen.

There is great irony and even humor in their action.

Can't you see the picture? They wanted the governor of the region, with all its political turmoil and intrigue, to assign a *guard at a graveyard!* The last place on earth you might expect to find a group of soldiers is in front of a tomb. But such was their request, for such was their fear. Conscience was digging away at the Pharisees, and they wanted nothing to upset them further.

Pilate had gone through enough trouble for any man to bear. He knew he was replaceable if he could not handle this Jesus matter well. He had already made a mess of the business of the trials which were a mockery. On the night before and the day of the crucifixion, Pilate kept handing off responsibility for Jesus, but He seemed to be a boomerang. The more Pilate sent Him away, the more He seemed to come back. Finally, in desperation Pilate washed his hands in a symbolic gesture that he was innocent of Jesus' blood. (See Matt. 27:24).

The visit of the Pharisees and chief priests on that sabbath day was probably the proverbial last straw as far as Pilate was concerned. Verses 65 and 66 of Matthew 27 present his words in a strident and contentious tone: "Take a guard,' Pilate answered. 'Go, make the tomb as secure as you know how.' So they went and made the tomb secure by putting a seal on the stone and posting the guard.' "

Pilate did not say to them to use the guard that they already had. The priests had a Temple guard. They were not the ones set up to guard the tomb. Pilate's emphasis would have been something like this: "You *have* a guard." That is, you have what you request. He sent his own soldiers to the tomb to make sure nothing else happened. Matthew used the Latin word *custodia* here. It suggested a contingent from the Roman army. Verse 14 of chapter 28 indicates that the soldiers were answerable to Pilate. The past two days had been hectic enough for Pilate, and he just did not want anything else to go wrong. The guard he sent were trusted soldiers who knew how to handle any situations which might have come up.

Pilate and the priests and Pharisees had become inextricably tied together in the death of Jesus. The religious leaders had relied on the power of Rome to quell the potentially disastrous religious revolution. Pilate relied on the power of the Temple to put down the potentially ruinous political upheaval. Jerusalem and Rome were married in a "shotgun" ceremony, and all the offspring were deformed.

The Jewish leaders took the Roman guard, sealed the tomb, and waited. Today people are still trying to seal that tomb, but are having no more success than the first attempt. It is simply no good. Good Friday had exposed the sham and pretense of power and religious formalism. The events of that Friday were not fair, but Christ never said life is fair.

Philip Yancy told of a priest who knew a doctor's family in Paraguay. This doctor spoke out against the human rights abuses of the military regime. To silence the doctor, the local police arrested his teenage son and tortured him to death. The people of the village where they had lived wanted to turn the funeral into a protest march, but the father chose another course of action. Instead of dressing the boy for the funeral, the doctor laid the boy out just as he had come from the prison. His naked body was full of bruises, scars from the electric shocks, and burns from cigarettes. The body was not laid out in a coffin but was laid on the blood-soaked mattress from the jail. Injustice was on public display.[1]

Yancy thought of this travesty in terms of Good Friday and Saturday when Jesus was silent in the tomb and wrote, "The Cross of Christ may have overcome evil, but it did not overcome unfairness. For that, Easter is required. Someday, God will restore all physical reality to its proper place under his reign. Until then, it is a good thing to remember that we live out our days on Easter Saturday.''[2]

That Saturday between the crucifixion and the resurrection was busy for the power brokers wanting to patch up the botched actions of the previous day and for the followers of Jesus who were trying to settle into a routine of anointing death and overcoming grief. But the tomb was silent. Much of our lives seem to be lived in this in-between time—not crucifixion but not resurrection. Perhaps the greatest act of faith is to go on in spite of the seeming silence from God.

Matthew presents the story of Saturday in such a way as to help readers sense the intrigue, the rage, and the fear which accompanied the events surrounding the death of Jesus. It was not a picnic! All the powers of darkness banded together to snuff out a light which shone in the blackness. George Buttrick put it this way:

> The sum of the Calvary story is this: men did their worst in wickedness, but it was not enough to defeat the power of God's love. They thought they had guaranteed the eclipse of Jesus in hatred and in shame. They killed Jesus and made the tomb secure. But it was not enough. He is the incarnate God, and it was not possible that death should hold him.[3]

Saturday: from God's Perspective

From the human perspective, Jesus' borrowed tomb seemed shrouded in an eerie silence on that Saturday. Jesus was dead, the followers were scattered, and a guard was in place. What was there to worry about?

From God's perspective, though, the silence of the grave was broken by some tremendous activity going on. That activity need not necessarily be thought of as literal activity or physical noises. There was a transaction, a happening, going on with God. The death of Christ was reconciling men to God and giving salvation for all who would accept that sacrificial death. If I were to choose just one word to sum up the meaning of Saturday, I would choose the word *forgiveness.*

Because of what Christ did on Friday—He gave His life— and on Saturday—His self-giving offering was accepted by God—the relationship between God and humans changed. I do not mean that God was brought close to humanity, but the other way around. Humanity was brought close to God. The cross of Christ genuinely changed the way people come to God. God says, "I forgive." That statement—"I forgive"—is at one and the same time the simplest good news ever announced and the most profound description of God's unfathomable mind. In Christ, God really forgives. Fisher Humphreys wrote:

> At the cross God in Christ bore the ultimate consequences of sin, thereby giving shape to divine forgiveness. When a man repents and trusts God, he is gloriously forgiven. This brings him under the conscious noncoercive influence of God. Whatever else God may be doing to transform the man, it is clear that in the setting of interpersonal relationship, forgiveness opens up relationships which lead to the sinner becoming a good man. These would include the man's gratitude, his new moral vision, his sense of being cleansed, his new understanding of God's costly love, the influence of God's love and goodness upon him, and most of all, his participation in the life of God and of God's people. No better hope for a sinner is conceivable, it seems to me, than that he should be forgiven by God in this costly way.[4]

George Bernard Shaw is reported to have said, "Forgiveness is a beggar's refuge—a man must pay his debts." Really? How are we to pay our debts? The good Mr. Shaw was mistaken, I think. God gives what we cannot provide, and His gift has the ability to transform even the most wretched person. Charles Wesley, one of the founders of Methodism, saw this happen when he preached to prisoners in London's infamous Newgate prison. Once he was preaching to ten men condemned to die. One of them, a black man who had robbed his master, heard this good news of forgiveness. Charles wrote, "I told him of one who came down from heaven to save lost sinners, and him in particular; described the sufferings of the Son of God, his sorrows, agony, and death. He listened with all the signs of eager astonishment; the tears trickled down his cheeks while he cried, 'What? Was it for me? Did he suffer all this for so poor a creature as me'?" When Wesley came back three days later he saw the obvious change in the prisoner who believed that God had forgiven him.

Wesley allowed himself to be locked in with the prisoners one evening before their execution. He led them in prayer and saw the fear and despair melt into peace and joy. A large crowd gathered at Tyburn the day of the hanging. When the cart carrying the condemned men drew up, Charles Wesley was there to meet it. He wrote, "The black spied me, coming out of the coach, and saluted me with his looks. As often as his eyes met mine, he smiled the most composed, delightful countenance I ever saw." A rope was placed over each man's head, and the moment of execution arrived. Wesley wrote, "When the cart drew off, not one struggled for life. We left them going to meet their Lord, ready for the Bridegroom. . . . I spoke a few suitable words to the crowd, and returned full of peace in our friends' happiness. That hour under the gallows was the most blessed hour of my life."[5] What could George Bernard Shaw have said of that?

Even if we could offer our lives, that would accomplish nothing which has not already been accomplished by Christ. When our country was still young, George Washington led a small group of men against various groups of

Indians who attacked isolated settlers. Some of the survivors of the burnings and scalpings went to Washington's headquarters to beg for his help. He wrote of this experience:

> The supplicating tears of the women and moving petitions of the men . . . melt me into such deadly sorrow that I solemnly declare, if I know my own mind, I could offer myself a willing sacrifice to the butchering enemy provided that would contribute to the people's ease. . . . If bleeding, dying! would glut their insatiate revenge, I would be a willing offering to savage fury, and die by inches to save a people.[6]

This is a noble gesture but one which would have had little effect because something would have been missing. That element is forgiveness. Jesus' sacrifice did not just vent hostile feelings or "glut their insatiate revenge." It puts people in an open stance before God, so they can appropriate His forgiveness and, in turn, forgive each other.

Henri Nouwen said, "Confession and forgiveness are the concrete forms in which we sinful people love one another."[7] I think he was exactly on target. Interaction between people is not always clear or positive. Relationships get clogged. Many families die from emotional hardening of the arteries. Many friendships are dashed to bits by unmet expectations and unrealistic hopes. Wherever two people are, there is also some amount of friction. Wayne Oates called this kind of friction "between-folks noise."[8] We might call forgiveness a lubricant which removes some of this friction or "noise." The only way to live together with others is to have some safety valve or pressure release which is part of what forgiveness is.

Hearing the Word Today

I have a close friend who did not see his father for fifteen years. The two did not communicate in any way during all that time because his parents had divorced. I had known that this disruption deeply affected my friend, but it was not until I was with both my friend and his father after their reconciliation that I saw some effects of the emotional vacuum. What a joy to watch them making up for lost time, to see the father beam at his son, and to watch the son return the admiration. It came about because they appropriated the gift of God called forgiveness.

Forgiveness is letting go of pain and its consequences. In a broader sense, it is the realization that the universe does not revolve around us. It is the insight that whatever slights and rebuffs which might come our way are really not very important in the long run. God has forgiven us in Christ. We are free to forgive others and to set relationships aright. We are free to see other people as needy, weak, and desperate, just like us. Erich Maria Remarque's novel *All Quiet on the Western Front* was based on his experience as a German soldier during the First World War. He described an incident in which he leaped into a foxhole and found it already occupied by an Englishman. Being in a close hole with the enemy terrified him at first, but he soon realized the British soldier had a terrible wound. The German was moved by his enemy's plight, so he gave the soldier a drink from his canteen. The wounded man indicated that he wanted Remarque to open his jacket pocket. When the German did, an envelope fell out. It contained pictures of his family, and the wounded man obviously wanted to see them once more before he died. The German soldier then held up the pictures of the Englishman's wife, children, and mother for him to see.

I am convinced that forgiveness begins at this level when

we realize, like the German soldier realized, that his enemy was a person like himself, with family, needs, dreams, and fears. The Englishman was a father, a husband, and a son. Two enemies met at a human level which surpassed political ideologies and nationalistic goals.

This experience is not just fiction. It happens in real life. David H. C. Read is a Presbyterian minister in New York City. He was a prisoner of war during the World War II. In his biography, *This Grace Given,* Read told about an experience he had in the POW camp one Christmas. He was something of an informal camp chaplain and represented the needs of his men to the Germans. These are Read's own words:

> The local commandant with whom I had to conduct official business was a fine old gentleman, a devout Christian. He did his best for us, and those in our party who were badly wounded were grateful. On Christmas Eve they made him a huge Christmas card and asked me to deliver it to him at midnight. I still can see him standing there in his office, lighting the last candle on an Advent wreath. I handed him the card. He was an erect and soldierly figure. He and I both knew that we were trying to do our duty by our country. My job was to wring concessions from him, help in escapes, and boost the morale of our troops while depressing that of the German guards. His job was to keep us firmly under control and to prevent escapes. We were at war. Yet there in the light of that Advent candle, as the bells of Rouen pealed the midnight hour, he looked at the card and the tears ran down his cheeks. Instinctively we shook hands. And there was a least a moment's armistice in that horrible war as we wished each other a Merry Christmas.[9]

Two men met as persons in the feeble light of an Advent candle and knew they were both subjects of the same Lord. That is the beginning of forgiveness. The forgiveness of Christ was made known on the Friday when He willingly went to a cross and on Saturday when He laid silent in the grave. His forgiveness changes us, and we help change each other as we pass it on.

Many people know about the killing of five missionaries in Ecuador in 1956. Members of the Auca Indians attacked and killed the missionaries who tried to tell the Aucas about Christ. Others finally managed to communicate with the Aucas and turned them to Christ. What makes this story so incredible is that the son of the pilot who died that January day went back to the region a decade later and was baptized by the very men who murdered his father! After the baptism, Stephen Saint and the Aucas went to the cemetery where Stephen's father, Nate Saint, along with Roger Youderian, Ed McCully, Pete Fleming, and Jim Elliot were buried. An Indian named Kimo prayed, "Father God, You know that the last time we came to this place we did wrong by killing these men. But now we know why they came here, and we know that one day we are going to meet these men in the sky whom we killed." Fifteen-year-old Stephen forgave the men who killed his father, and he himself was changed.[10]

Yes, that is what Saturday of Easter week teaches. As we forgive, so are we forgiven. God has already initiated the process, but He leaves the next step to us. Ready for a little journey?

Notes

1. Philip Yancy, "Saturday Seven Days a Week," *Christianity Today*, 18 March 1988, 64.

2. Philip Yancy, *Disappointment with God: Three Questions No One Asks Aloud* (Grand Rapids: Zondervan Publishing House, 1988), 186.

3. George A. Buttrick, *The Interpreter's Bible* (New York: Abingdon Press, 1951), 7:614-15.

4. Fisher Humphreys, *The Death of Christ* (Nashville: Broadman Press,

1978), 162. (This book is now published by Insight Press of New Orleans.)

5. These words of Wesley are gathered in a biography by Arnold A. Dallimore, *A Heart Set Free: the Life of Charles Wesley* (Westchester, Ill: Crossway Books, 1988), 71-73.

6. Washington, quoted in James Hightower, comp., *Illustrating The Gospel of Matthew.* (Nashville: Broadman Press, 1982), 106.

7. Henri J. M. Nouwen, *In Jesus' Name: Reflections on Christian Leadership* (New York: Crossroad Publishing Company, 1989), 46.

8. Wayne E. Oates, *Nurturing Silence in a Noisy Heart.* (Garden City: Doubleday & Company, 1979), 12.

9. David H. C. Read, *This Grace Given.* (Grand Rapids: Eerdmans Publishing Co., 1984), 117.

10. Stephen Saint, as told to Dan Wooding, "Baptized By the Men Who Murdered My Father," *Decision,* September 1986, 14-15.

8

SUNDAY

Easter Joy

It was Friday. The cynics were lookin' at the world and sayin', "as things have been so they shall be. You can't change anything in this world, you can't change anything." But those cynics didn't know that it was only Friday. Sunday's comin'! —Tony Campolo

I have stood at three graves which point out much of human beings' grandeur and folly. Two of the graves are of men who, in their time, were two of the most powerful men in the world. The first was that of Winston Churchill. His grave is a short distance from Blenheim Place near Oxford, England. Carla and I visited the Buckingham Palace and were impressed with its magnitude and its elaborate decor. Based on that, I had expected that Churchill's grave would be something equally magnificent. When we found it, I was both surprised and a little disappointed. What struck me about it was the fact that it was so small and unpretentious. It looked fairly ordinary and nothing like what I expected. It was in a small plot with just a few other graves around and looked much like the final resting place of any other man.

Another grave I visited was that of Harry S. Truman in Independence, Missouri. Like that of Churchill's, Truman's grave is not very elaborate or large. It is located on the grounds of his presidential library and is well kept but not ornate. Again, I felt a sense of letdown when I saw it.

After all, Truman, along with Churchill and Joseph Stalin, were three of the most powerful men during the end of World War II. Churchill led England during the awful days of the German bombings. Truman became president of the United States after the death of Franklin Roosevelt. He made the decision to use atomic weapons on Japan. Two powerful men—Truman and Churchill—and two small and ordinary graves.

The third grave which so impressed me was of a man who was known for his fried chicken business. He had a huge monument which seemed to stand guard over his tomb. A casual observer who did not know who he was might have mistaken him for a president, or at least a governor. But a chicken entrepreneur?

The contrast between the final resting places of the two world leaders and the businessman is both striking and instructive. Two were content to let their actions serve as their monument. The other wanted to have something more concrete—literally. Which will actually live in the minds of others longer? Only time will tell, but I am sure that Churchill and Truman will outlast the chicken king. The latter would have been instructed by the wisdom of Eduard Benes. Dr. Benes was the foreign minister in the cabinet of Thomas Masaryk, the first president of Czechoslovakia when it came into existence in 1918. Benes is buried in Lany, a town about twenty-five miles outside Prague. His grave, along with those of three Masaryks, is unmarked. Shortly before his death, Benes told a friend why he wanted an unmarked grave: "If the people love me, I shall live in their hearts and they will never forget the place of my grave; hence an identification is unnecessary. If they do not love me, I shall be forgotten in their hearts; and the most elaborate tombstone will make no difference."

Many people like to be able to point to the final resting place of their leader and say, "This is his monument. Isn't it magnificent?" Elvis lovers have Graceland, for example. But what do the followers of Jesus have? The fact is that Easter was a day of the unmarked grave. The only things which Jesus left behind which could be considered any sort of monument were a rugged cross, an empty tomb, and a living church. Even so, some Christians would like for the resurrection to have been a day of pomp and circumstance, a production which would have shamed Cecil B. DeMille. They might like for it to have been an event like the launching of Friendship 7, the space capsule which took John Glenn into space in February 20, 1962. Alister Cooke said that this was such a public event that everybody watched— everybody! The New York police reported that for twenty minutes during the launch, not one phone call came into police headquarters. Even crime took a brief respite.

God chose to do things very differently. No one even saw the resurrection happen. Some of Jesus' followers saw the signs of it—an empty tomb, grave clothes, an angelic vision, and later appearances by the risen Lord. No eyewitness were on hand when it happened, however. Despite that fact, generations of Christians have believed the reports and have endeavored to follow the living Christ. A curious fact is that for many of even the most devout Christians, the major holiday of the church is not Easter but is Christmas. The reason may be that for many people Good Friday and its grisly reality and the mystery of Easter are not as personal and inviting as Christmas. Jesus' death on a cross, His time spent in a dark tomb, and the sunrise surprise of Easter just do not grab many people at the same emotional level as bright lights, annual carols, gift giving, and eggnog by the fireplace. So what is Easter?

The New Testament Witness

Easter was a day that changed everything. The account of this day in the New Testament is presented as a witness by people who were changed because of Easter. In 1 Corinthians 15 Paul gave the first account of the meaning of the resurrection. His description is given is summary form:

> For what I received I passed on to you as of first importance: that Christ died for our sins according to the Scriptures, that he was buried, that he was raised on the third day according to the Scriptures, and that he appeared to Peter, and then to the Twelve. After that, he appeared to more than five hundred of the brothers at the same time, most of whom are still living, though some have fallen asleep. Then he appeared to James, then to all the apostles, and last of all he appeared to me also, as to one abnormally born (vv. 3-8).

In such a short space, Paul summed up the events of Easter and afterward. In the rest of 1 Corinthians 15, he spelled out what Christ's resurrection means to us. In short, it is assurance and power for living now and the promise of eternal life with Christ later. In a sense, followers of Christ gamble all on His resurrection. We stand or fall with Him. As Paul put it, "If only for this life we have hope in Christ, we are to be pitied more than all men" (v. 19).

The apostle was convinced that Easter was a day that changed everything. Because of what God did in Christ, life and eternity would not be the same. Mark Twain told of the night the Mississippi River cut through a narrow neck of land and changed courses. A Negro went to sleep as a slave in Missouri. He awoke to discover that because of the river's change, the land he was in was Illinois, and he was a free man.[1] One day changed everything for the man. I think this is true with Easter. Because of the events of that day and the meaning which God attached to them, everyone who would say yes to Christ would be different.

The Gospel accounts of the resurrection give more details about that event. John 20 gives one of the clearest pictures of the surprise and joy of Easter. The day did not begin with joy, however. "No one ever told me that grief felt so like fear." These are the words which C. S. Lewis used as the opener for the book about his wife's death, *A Grief Observed.* The disciples of Jesus, and especially Mary Magdalene, could have supplied that line. They knew personally that grief and fear are Siamese twins.

Mary went early on Sunday morning to the tomb where Jesus had been laid. The end of John 19 indicates that the burial of Jesus in the tomb of Joseph was temporary. The Jewish Passover was about to begin at sundown on Friday, so the authorities were anxious to get rid of the bodies from public view. Joseph and Nicodemus took Jesus' body and laid it in a grave after a quick preparation (19:39-42). Joseph sealed the tomb with a large stone. The Jewish authorities then placed a guard at the tomb.

Mary went to the tomb before daybreak on the first day of the week. Sunday was for the Jews what Monday is for modern Americans. Why did she go? We cannot be certain, but there are several good possible answers. She was personally devoted to Jesus, and His death on the previous Friday had shattered Mary emotionally. She went back to the grave as a symbol of her love and devotion. Whatever else she might have brought with her, Mary surely brought deep feelings of grief and hopelessness. Death is never a pleasant subject, especially when it comes is such a gruesome fashion as on that Friday. Most people fear death, and some will not even discuss it. Claudia in Shakespeare's *Measure for Measure* said:

> The weariest and most loathed worldly life
> That age, ache, penury, and imprisonment
> Can lay on nature, is a paradise
> To what we fear of death.

On the first Easter, Mary stalked death. As she got to the tomb, she saw that the stone which Joseph had placed at the entrance was rolled back. This was insult added to injury. Not only had Jesus' enemies killed Him but also they apparently had stolen His body. Mary was sad, despairing, and confused about the whole affair.

In that regard, Mary was like multitudes of people today who live with hopeless hearts and dashed dreams. A pastor I know about moved to a new church field. He was invited to lunch by a widow in the congregation. He went to the home on the agreed date and was surprised to find three places set. He learned that this woman had been widowed for seventeen years, yet she still set a place for her former husband and continually talked about him during the meal. The pastor had his job cut out for him as he tried to bring this lady out of her self-exile in grief into the land of the living.

We can be sympathetic with this lady, and we can understand Mary Magdalene's turmoil as she found the tomb of Jesus empty. Mary had a conversation with two angels at that place. From her tone and movement of the conversation, we can surmise that she did not know they were angels. They asked why she was crying. Her reply was poignant and moving: "They have taken my Lord away, and I don't know where they have put him."

Mary's dashed dreams and hopeless outlook had not yet been changed by an encounter with the One for whom Easter is remembered. She still thought the Son of God was dead! In the 1960s a movement swept across the country which proclaimed confidently, "God is dead." But that movement is now dead, and people still look to Easter as a lighthouse in a storm.

Some modern people feel as hopeless about life as Mary did. Some singles want a loving and lasting relationship but seem to have trouble establishing it. Some adults feel trapped in their jobs. Some teenagers think that life is a bad joke, and they end their own lives. It is to such as these, as well as to the rest of us, that the good news of Easter is directed. Not everyone, though, can see or experience this good news without some help. One of the reasons churches exist is to help people find meaning in life as interpreted through Easter faith. Such faith is a filter which effects every claim to truth and every action. If the tomb was emptied because of God, life takes on a very different meaning than if enemies simply stole Jesus' body.

Mary went to the tomb overwhelmed with grief and hopelessness. She was not in an emotional state at first to "see" what had occurred. To her the angels seemed to be passersby, and she mistook the risen Christ for the gardener. Through her tears and the dark veil over her mental state, Mary just could not recognize whom she saw. The eyes of faith are needed to penetrate through the fog of grief. Not only that, but a special way of looking at life is needed. Easter joy is not apparent to many people. They must be taught to "see" what is not openly evident to everyone. I do not mean that we deceive others or ourselves but rather that we penetrate below the surface of life. Theseus in Shakespeare's *A Midsummer Night's Dream* said:

> Lovers and madmen have such seething brains,
> Such shaping fantasies, that apprehended
> More than cool reason ever comprehends.
> The lunatic, the lover, and the poet
> Are of imagination all compact.

Yes, lovers of Christ really do apprehend something of great significance in His resurrection. Even so, some people today live with such crushing circumstances that their senses are dulled. They have a tough time sensing spiritual reality. They need help to break through the veil of darkness which envelopes them. Part of what Easter signifies is this breaking through to an inner sense of insight.

What a time it must have been for Mary! She had gone to the tomb despairing over the loss of her closest friend. Then she had been further disheartened to find His body gone from its tomb. Further, she was encountered by two unknown people, and then another who wanted to know who she was looking for.

Then, in the midst of all this, Jesus spoke her name— "Mary"—and she knew Him. She was then given a task: go and tell. Her witness to the other followers of Jesus is recorded in John 20:18: "Mary of Magdala went to the disciples with the news: 'I have seen the Lord!' And she told them that he had said these things to her."

Mary was given something to do. She was to be a witness. She had no special status and no education. Mary was an ordinary woman who had an extraordinary experience. That was enough to send her to others saying, "I have seen the Lord!"

The empty tomb and the meeting with Jesus gave her hope. Today's believers' relationship with Christ is based on faith and not touch. Our faith in Christ and His mission gives us the hope which Mary found in the garden. It also gives us the courage to share our faith with others. To witness means precisely what Mary did. It is not telling others about secondhand knowledge or hearsay evidence. When a person witnesses, he or she is saying in effect, "I have experienced the risen Lord. Let me tell you about my experience." You cannot prove anything about your faith. If it were provable, it would not be faith. (See Heb. 11:1.) Easter is, thus, not about proof, but it is about coming into a relationship with Christ who is not subject to the grave.

Belief in the resurrection undergoes changes and shifts of attitudes in some fellowships. A biographer of British writer Dorothy L. Sayers has noted how the attitude about the resurrection changed in the Church of England during Dorothy's life. When she was a child, a bishop who doubted the resurrection was thought of a being courageous. When Dorothy was a girl, G. K. Chesterton said that he believed in the resurrection, and people called him "odd." When the writer went off to Oxford University, people who believed in the resurrection were called advanced. By the time Sayers was middle-aged, people who believed in the resurrection were called courageous. Finally, when she was older, people who, like herself, wrote about Christianity and the resurrection were called escapists and bullies. People who attacked her were called courageous for doing so.[2] Though attitudes and opinions might shift and spin like a weather vane in a storm, all the critics in the world cannot discredit Christ's resurrection. I believe that He literally arose from the dead and that His renewed life was a promise of things to come. It also pointed out something wonderful about God.

God of the Breakthrough

On Easter, Christ broke out of the seeming permanence of death. That breakthrough was a sign of what lies in store for any who will come to Christ as a follower. It was also a sign of the ability of God to break through every form of barrier, hindrance, and grave that stands in His way. This happens in our lives when we accept Him. It happens when God gets "under the skin" of even the most outward pagan. When George Bush was vice president of the United States, one of his official duties was to represent our country at the funeral of Soviet leader Brezhnev. The entire funeral procession was marked by its military precision. There was a coldness and hollowness which enveloped it. Since the Soviet Union is officially atheistic, no comforting prayers or spiritual hymns were sung. Only the marching soldiers, steel helmets, and Marxist rhetoric were offered. There was no mention of God. Mr. Bush was close to the casket when Mrs. Brezhnev came for her last good-bye. Bush said, "She walked up, took one last look at her husband and there—in the cold, gray center of that totalitarian state, she traced the sign of the cross on her husband's chest. I was stunned. In that simple act, God had broken through the core of the communist system."[3] That act stuns me, too, but I realize that no system can wall God out just as no tomb can wall God in. Evil had its day on Friday, but Sunday was coming.

A story tells about the great cosmic struggle between the forces of evil and the power of good. The story says that God, as everybody knows, created the heavens and earth and everything in them. He created them by His words because words are power. God said, "Let there be light," and there was light. This happened with everything. God was rightly proud of His work, but especially proud of man and woman which He made. He even breathed life into them.

Now the devil was jealous and angry. One day when God was enjoying the man and woman, the devil walked by casually. He slithered up to God and asked him why He liked those strange human creatures so much. God opened His mouth to speak, and the devil craftily put a bond upon His tongue. God could not speak, not even one word! Since God's creative power was in His words, the sly old devil had bound His power.

The devil laughed at God and then proceeded to have his way with the man and the woman. Aeons went by, and the devil came back to taunt God. He scoffed at the silent God and mocked Him. God responded to this by holding up one finger. "One?" asked the devil. "Are you telling me that you want to say just one word?" God nodded. The devil, being both crafty and confident, thought, "I suppose that even God could not do much with just one word. OK." So the devil removed the bond from God's tongue. Then God spoke His one word is a quiet whisper. He spoke it for the man and the woman, and it brought them great joy. It was a word that gathered up all the forgiveness, love, and creativity God had stored up in His heart during His long silence. His one word was "Jesus."[4]

That is what Easter is all about! It reminds me of a very old way of thinking about that day. It goes this way:

> God played chess with the devil
> And the pieces were human beings.
> The devil was ahead
> Until God became one of the pieces.
> "Check," said the devil at Golgotha.
> Three days later
> God replied, "Checkmate."

The empty tomb is a symbol of hope—the hope that is ours when God says, "Checkmate." It is a hope that comes our way when we live as part of the family of God.

Results of His Sacrifice

In 1977 a man named Jean Bedel Bokassa, a former French paratrooper, proclaimed himself emperor of the Central African Republic. This new nation was founded in 1960 and had a population of two million people. It was listed among the twenty-five poorest nations. The average annual income was $155 when Bokassa took over. Even so, he held an inaugural gala that cost $30 million! He had a six-foot diamond-encrusted scepter, a twenty-four-foot red velvet cape, and a two-ton gold-plated throne. His 2,000 guests were served hundreds of pounds of caviar and 24,-000 bottles of champagne, all flown in by charted plane from France. Despite the poverty of "his people" and the extravagance of his coronation, Bokassa was quoted as saying, "One cannot create a great history without sacrifices."[5] True enough, but who made the sacrifice?

Jesus' life, public ministry, willingness to face death, and resurrection are of a nature so very different from this African usurper. When He was ready to sacrifice for His people, Jesus did not squander the little which they had. Instead, He gave Himself as the sacrifice. His life was real, and His beatings and crucifixion were also real. I have a catalogue of Christian costumes for use in church dramas. One item in this catalog under the Easter heading is listed as, "Whip scars: 6 assorted-length scars." Also listed are "hand scars" and a "crown of thorns." All of these come complete with cement which will attach these rubber "scars" to an actor. Jesus had no make-believe welts, nor did He bleed stage makeup. What He offered on the cross was fully and essentially Himself, and what was raised on Easter was fully and essentially Himself also.

The effect of this genuine sacrifice and resurrection is that we are now reconciled—brought together—with God. As Paul said in 2 Corinthians 5:21, "God made him who had no sin to be sin for us, so that in him we might become the righteousness of God." Out of Christ's brokenness came life, not just for Himself on Easter, but for all who take His promise as their own.

After the Second World War, much of Berlin was in ruins. The Germans decided to pile the shattered bricks, twisted steel, and broken stones in one place and made a huge mountain out of it. They laid topsoil over the pile and seeded it with grass and planted trees. Today families can picnic on its glens, and in winter people sled down the slopes. They built something good over the ruins of destruction.[6]

Easter is something like that. God took the worst men could do, and He brought something wonderful out of it. As I consider this great reversal, I remember that the Bible is full of that sort of thing. Adam and Eve made a mess of things, but God still protected them. Abraham wavered and

Sarah laughed, but God still guided them. Isaac was a weak leader, but God used him anyway. Jacob was a trickster and manipulator, but God worked out His plan through Him. Moses murdered, and his people murmured, but God brought good out of it. The personnel file of the Bible is not populated with "supersaints" who are flawless but with genuine flesh-and-blood people with glaring faults. Through them God works out His grand scheme. What God began in the garden of Eden He brought to fruition by way of an empty tomb which quietly proclaims God's control.

Hearing The Word Today

On that first Easter some people believed, but some doubted. That situation has not changed much as far as I can tell. Philip Yancey said this of Jesus and Easter:

> The three events—birth, death, and resurrection—were surely tremors in the cosmos. Yet, carried out so mysteriously, with such a strange assortment of witnesses, they forever complicated faith. They gave just enough reason to believe for those who, like the disciples, chose faith, and just enough reason not to believe for those who, like the Roman guards, chose doubt. That, too, has not changed since Jesus' time. [7]

On Easter God said, "I forgive. Now you may forgive too." We Christians are people who are sandwiched in between the open hand of God on one side and the closed fist of people on the other. The trick is to find ways of opening those fists and putting them into the open hand which awaits them. So we learn forgiveness and reconciliation.

Ira Sankey was a gospel singer who gained national recognition as he traveled with evangelist Dwight L. Moody. Sankey performed one Christmas Eve for passen-

gers on a steamer on the Delaware River. One of the pass-
engers recognized Sankey's voice from an experience during the Civil War. This man approached to the singer and
asked if he had ever been in the army. The singer did not
recognize this man and thought he might be a traveling
salesman. Sankey replied that he had joined the Union
army in 1860. The stranger asked, "I wonder if you can
remember back to 1862. Did you ever do guard duty, at
night, in Maryland?" Sankey replied that he had pulled
such duty at Sharpsburg. The other man said, "I was in the
army, too—the Confederate army. I saw you that night."
Sankey looked at him warily.

The man explained that he had seen Sankey parading in
his blue uniform. He put Sankey in his rifle sights as his
form was silhouetted by a full moon. Just as the Rebel
soldier was ready to squeeze off a shot, Sankey began to
sing. The stranger said, "You sang the same song you sang
tonight, 'Savior Like a Shepherd Lead Us'." Sankey said, "I
remember!" The stranger continued, "My mother sang
that song a lot, but I never expected no soldier to be singing it at midnight, on guard duty. Especially a Union Soldier." The man sighed, "Obviously I didn't shoot you."
Sankey smiled and said, "And obviously I'm grateful."

"I always wondered who you were. Who it was I didn't
kill that night on account of his singing an old Sunday
School song. Frankly, up until tonight, the name Ira Sankey
wouldn't have meant much to me. Guess I don't read the
paper like I should. I didn't know you'd turn out to be so
famous! But I reckon I would have recognized the voice
and the song anyplace." Sankey thought about what might
have been. The man said, "Do you think we could talk a
mite? I think you owe it to me. Very little has gone right for
me. Not before the war. Not during it. And not since." Ira
Sankey put his arm around his former enemy and led him
off to a quiet corner where he could tell him about a Man

who was killed by His enemies but who arose from the grave.[8]

Easter seems to indicate that everything good comes from a crucible. Evil forces combine and try to exile God from His world. But out of the crucible of the cross and the grave arises a new life and a new word. The angel at the empty tomb said, "He is not here; he has risen!" Because that is true, people are brought together with other people and with God. That fact is the long and the short of the Easter story. The eight days that changed the world began with Jesus' entry into Jerusalem and ended with His exit from a clammy tomb. Because of His triumph, we who love Him need not fear the stranglehold of doubt and death.

Peter wrote, "We have the word of the prophets made more certain, and you will do well to pay attention to it, as to a light shining in a dark place, until the day dawns and the morning star rises in your heart" (2 Pet. 1:19). That Morning Star arose from the grave and is now rising in the hearts of those who love Him. The inscription in the crypt of the Allegheny Observatory at the University of Pittsburgh is instructive for us: "We have loved the stars too fondly to be fearsome of the night."

Yes, we have.

Notes

1. This story comes from Dr. Joe E. Trull, *Proclaim*, July-September 1988, 36.

2. Alzina Stone Dale, *Maker and Craftsman: The Story of Dorothy L. Sayers.* (Grand Rapids: Eerdmans, 1978), 37.

3. George Bush, quoted in *Christianity Today*, 16 October 1987, 37.

4. William J. Bausch, *Story Telling: Faith and Imagination* (Mystic, Conn.: Twenty-Third Publications, 1984), 115-116.

5. Fritz Ridenour, *How to Decide Lord, What's Really Important* (Ventura, Calif: Regal Books, 1978), 23-24. The story is from the *Los Angeles Times*.

6. This story is told by Roy L. Honeycutt in "The Tie," July/August 1987, 16.

7. Philip Yancey, "The Most Surprising Miracle of All," *Christianity Today,* 4 April 1986, 64.

8. John Gillies, "Mr. Sankey Celebrates Christmas," *Christian Herald.* December 1978, 16. The story is retold in David S. McCarthy, *Practical Guide for the Christian Writer* (Valley Forge: Judson Press, 1983), 78-79.